필사 영어로 배우는

지혜의 책 잠언

저자: 서 미 미

도서출판보혜

서 문

필사와 필기의 개념을 먼저 생각을 하려고 합니다.
필사는 말 그대로 글씨 위에 글씨를 따라 그리는 형태를 말하고 필기는 글씨를 받아 적거나 글을 보고 백지면 위에 글씨를 쓰는 형태를 말합니다.
이 책은 제목처럼 필사입니다.
왼쪽은 필기체이며, 오른쪽은 인쇄체입니다.
몇 단어씩 보게 하여 쓰게 하였습니다.

필사 연습을 하면 처음에는 모방을 하는 듯 하지만 오랜 시간이 지나면 자신도 모르는 사이에 자신만의 필체를 만들어가며 생활에서 마음 속 깊이 자부심이 심어지고 인내력과 정신력이 깊이 향상되어 가는 것을 깨닫게 될 것입니다.

혼자 있는 시간에 장소가 어디가 되었든 필사를 하면서 말씀이 주는 위로를 통해 마음에 심지가 견고하여지는 평화가 있기를 바랍니다.

더불어 《필사 영어로 배우는 지혜의 책 잠언》을 통하여 믿음 안에서 지혜도 얻고 영어 실력이 한층 성장하는 기회가 되기를 기원합니다.

서 미 미 올 림

필사 영어로 배우는 지혜의 책 목록표

Proberbs 1

1:1
The proverbs of Solomon, son of David, king of Israel:

1:2
That men may know wisdom and instruction, understand words of insight,

1:3
receive instruction in wise dealing, righteousness, justice, and equity;

1:4
that prudence may be given to the simple, knowledge and discretion to the youth-

Proberbs 1

1:1
The proverbs of Solomon, son of David, king of Israel:

1:2
That men may know wisdom and instruction, understand words of insight,

1:3
receive instruction in wise dealing, righteousness, justice, and equity;

1:4
that prudence may be given to the simple, knowledge and discretion to the youth-

1:5

the wise man also may hear and increase in learning, and the man of understanding acquire skill,

1:6

to understand a proverb and a figure, the words of the wise and their riddles.

1:7

The fear of the LORD is the beginning of knowledge; fools despise wisdom and instruction.

1:5
the wise man also may hear and increase in learning, and the man of understanding acquire skill,

1:6
to understand a proverb and a figure, the words of the wise and their riddles.

1:7
The fear of the LORD is the beginning of knowledge; fools despise wisdom and instruction.

1:8
Hear, my son, your father's instruction, and reject not your mother's teaching;

1:9
for they are a fair garland for your head, and pendants for your neck.

1:10
My son, if sinners entice you, do not consent.

1:11
If they say, "Come with us, let us lie in wait for blood, let us wantonly

1:8
Hear, my son, your father's instruction, and reject not your mother's teaching;

1:9
for they are a fair garland for your head, and pendants for your neck.

1:10
My son, if sinners entice you, do not consent.

1:11
If they say, "Come with us, let us lie in wait for blood, let us wantonly

ambush the innocent;

1:12
like Sheol let us swallow them alive and whole, like those who go down to the Pit;

1:13
we shall find all precious goods, we shall fill our houses with spoil;

1:14
throw in your lot among us, we will all have one purse" -

ambush the innocent;

1:12
like Sheol let us swallow them alive and whole, like those who go down to the Pit;

1:13
we shall find all precious goods, we shall fill our houses with spoil;

1:14
throw in your lot among us, we will all have one purse" -

1:15

my son, do not walk in the way with them, hold back your foot from their paths;

1:16

for their feet run to evil, and they make haste to shed blood.

1:17

For in vain is a net spread in the sight of any bird;

1:18

but these men lie in wait for their own blood, they set an ambush

1:15
my son, do not walk in the way with them, hold back your foot from their paths;

1:16
for their feet run to evil, and they make haste to shed blood.

1:17
For in vain is a net spread in the sight of any bird;

1:18
but these men lie in wait for their own blood, they set an ambush

for their own lives.

1:19

Such are the ways of all who get gain by violence; it takes away the life of its possessors.

1:20

Wisdom cries aloud in the street; in the markets she raises her voice;

1:21

on the top of the walls she cries out; at the entrance of the city gates she speaks:

for their own lives.

1:19

Such are the ways of all who get gain by violence; it takes away the life of its possessors.

1:20

Wisdom cries aloud in the street; in the markets she raises her voice;

1:21

on the top of the walls she cries out; at the entrance of the city gates she speaks:

1:22

"How long, O simple ones,
will you love being simple?
How long will scoffers
delight in their scoffing and
fools hate knowledge?

1:23

Give heed to my reproof;
behold, I will pour out my
thoughts to you;
I will make my words
known to you.

1:24

Because I have called and

1:22
"How long, O simple ones, will you love being simple? How long will scoffers delight in their scoffing and fools hate knowledge?

1:23
Give heed to my reproof; behold, I will pour out my thoughts to you; I will make my words known to you.

1:24
Because I have called and

you refused to listen, have stretched out my hand and no one has heeded,

1:25
and you have ignored all my counsel and would have none of my reproof,

1:26
I also will laugh at your calamity; I will mock when panic strikes you,

1:27
when panic strikes you like a storm, and your calamity comes like a whirlwind, when distress

you refused
to listen, have
stretched out
my hand
and no one
has heeded,

1:25
and you have
ignored all my
counsel and
would have
none of my
reproof,

1:26
I also will
laugh at your
calamity; I will
mock when
panic strikes
you,

1:27
when panic
strikes you
like a storm,
and your
calamity
comes like a
whirlwind,
when distress

and anguish come upon you.

1:28

Then they will call upon me, but I will not answer; they will seek me diligently but will not find me.

1:29

Because they hated knowledge and did not choose the fear of the LORD,

1:30

would have none of my counsel, and despised all my reproof,

and anguish come upon you.

1:28
Then they will call upon me, but I will not answer; they will seek me diligently but will not find me.

1:29
Because they hated knowledge and did not choose the fear of the LORD,

1:30
would have none of my counsel, and despised all my reproof,

1:31

therefore they shall eat the fruit of their way and be sated with their own devices.

1:32

For the simple are killed by their turning away, and the complacence of fools destroys them;

1:33

but he who listens to me will dwell secure and will be at ease, without dread of evil."

1:31
therefore they shall eat the fruit of their way and be sated with their own devices.

1:32
For the simple are killed by their turning away, and the complacence of fools destroys them;

1:33
but he who listens to me will dwell secure and will be at ease, without dread of evil."

Proverbs 2

2:1
My son, if you receive my words and treasure up my commandments with you,

2:2
making your ear attentive to wisdom and inclining your heart to understanding;

2:3
yes, if you cry out for insight and raise your voice for understanding,

2:4
if you seek it like silver

Proverbs 2

2:1
My son, if you receive my words and treasure up my commandments with you,

2:2
making your ear attentive to wisdom and inclining your heart to understanding;

2:3
yes, if you cry out for insight and raise your voice for understanding,

2:4
if you seek it like silver

and search for it as for hidden treasures;

2:5
then you will understand the fear of the LORD and find the knowledge of God.

2:6
For the LORD gives wisdom; from his mouth come knowledge and understanding;

2:7
he stores up sound wisdom for the upright; he is a shield to those who walk in integrity,

and search for it as for hidden treasures;

2:5
then you will understand the fear of the LORD and find the knowledge of God.

2:6
For the LORD gives wisdom; from his mouth come knowledge and understanding;

2:7
he stores up sound wisdom for the upright; he is a shield to those who walk in integrity,

2:8
guarding the paths of justice and preserving the way of his saints.

2:9
Then you will understand righteousness and justice and equity, every good path;

2:10
for wisdom will come into your heart, and knowledge will be pleasant to your soul;

2:11
discretion will watch over you; understanding will

2:8
guarding the paths of justice and preserving the way of his saints.

2:9
Then you will understand righteousness and justice and equity, every good path;

2:10
for wisdom will come into your heart, and knowledge will be pleasant to your soul;

2:11
discretion will watch over you; understanding will

guard you;

2:12

delivering you from the way of evil, from men of perverted speech,

2:13

who forsake the paths of uprightness to walk in the ways of darkness,

2:14

who rejoice in doing evil and delight in the perverseness of evil;

2:15

men whose paths are

guard you;

2:12
delivering you from the way of evil, from men of perverted speech,

2:13
who forsake the paths of uprightness to walk in the ways of darkness,

2:14
who rejoice in doing evil and delight in the perverseness of evil;

2:15
men whose paths are

crooked, and who are devious in their ways.

2:16

You will be saved from the loose woman, from the adventuress with her smooth words,

2:17

who forsakes the companion of her youth and forgets the covenant of her God ;

2:18

for her house sinks down to death, and her paths to the shades;

crooked, and who are devious in their ways.

2:16
You will be saved from the loose woman, from the adventuress with her smooth words,

2:17
who forsakes the companion of her youth and forgets the covenant of her God;

2:18
for her house sinks down to death, and her paths to the shades;

2:19
none who go to her come back nor do they regain the paths of life.

2:20
So you will walk in the way of good men and keep to the paths of the righteous.

2:21
For the upright will inhabit the land, and men of integrity will remain in it;

2:22
but the wicked will be cut off from the land, and the treacherous will be rooted out of it.

2:19
none who go to her come back nor do they regain the paths of life.

2:20
So you will walk in the way of good men and keep to the paths of the righteous.

2:21
For the upright will inhabit the land, and men of integrity will remain in it;

2:22
but the wicked will be cut off from the land, and he treacherous will be rooted out of it.

Proberbs 3

3:1
My son, do not forget my teaching, but let your heart keep my commandments;

3:2
for length of days and years of life and abundant welfare will they give you.

3:3
Let not loyalty and faithfulness forsake you; bind them about your neck, write them on the tablet of your heart.

Proberbs 3

3:1
My son, do not forget my teaching, but let your heart keep my commandments;

3:2
for length of days and years of life and abundant welfare will they give you.

3:3
Let not loyalty and faithfulness forsake you; bind them about your neck, write them on the tablet of your heart.

3:4
So you will find favor and good repute in the sight of God and man.

3:5
Trust in the LORD with all your heart, and do not rely on your own insight.

3:6
In all your ways acknowledge him, and he will make straight your paths.

3:7
Be not wise in your own eyes; fear the LORD, and turn away from evil.

3:4
So you will find favor and good repute in the sight of God and man.

3:5
Trust in the LORD with all your heart, and do not rely on your own insight.

3:6
In all your ways acknowledge him, and he will make straight your paths.

3:7
Be not wise in your own eyes; fear the LORD, and turn away from evil.

3:8
It will be healing to your flesh and refreshment to your bones.
3:9
Honor the LORD with your substance and with the first fruits of all your produce;
3:10
then your barns will be filled with plenty, and your vats will be bursting with wine.
3:11
My son, do not despise the LORD's discipline or be weary of his reproof,

3:8
It will be
healing to
your flesh and
refreshment
to your
bones.
3:9
Honor the
LORD with
your substance
and with the
first fruits of
all your
produce;
3:10
then your
barns will be
filled with
plenty, and
your vats will
be bursting
with wine.

3:11
My son, do
not despise
the LORD's
discipline or
be weary of
his reproof,

3:12
for the LORD reproves him whom he loves, as a father the son in whom he delights.
3:13
Happy is the man who finds wisdom,
and the man who gets understanding,
3:14
for the gain from it is better than gain from silver and its profit better than gold.
3:15
She is more precious than jewels, and nothing you

3:12
for the LORD reproves him whom he loves, as a father the son in whom he delights.

3:13
Happy is the man who finds wisdom, and the man who gets understanding.

3:14
for the gain from it is better than gain from silver and its profit better than gold.

3:15
She is more precious than jewels, and nothing you

desire can compare with her.

3:16

Long life is in her right hand; in her left hand are riches and honor.

3:17

Her ways are ways of pleasantness, and all her paths are peace.

3:18

She is a tree of life to those who lay hold of her; those who hold her fast are called happy.

3:19

The LORD by wisdom founded the earth; by

desire can compare with her.

3:16
Long life is in her right hand; in her left hand are riches and honor.

3:17
Her ways are ways of pleasantness, and all her paths are peace.

3:18
She is a tree of life to those who lay hold of her; those who hold her fast are called happy.

3:19
The LORD by wisdom founded the earth; by

understanding he established the heavens;

3:20

by his knowledge the deeps broke forth, and the clouds drop down the dew.

3:21

My son, keep sound wisdom and discretion; let them not escape from your sight,

3:22

and they will be life for your soul and adornment for your neck.

3:23

Then you will walk on your way securely and

understanding he established the heavens;

3:20

by his knowledge the deeps broke forth, and the clouds drop down the dew.

3:21

My son, keep sound wisdom and discretion; let them not escape from your sight,

3:22

and they will be life for your soul and adornment for your neck.

3:23

Then you will walk on your way securely and

your foot will not stumble.

3:24

If you sit down, you will not be afraid; when you lie down, your sleep will be sweet.

3:25

Do not be afraid of sudden panic, or of the ruin of the wicked, when it comes;

3:26

for the LORD will be your confidence and will keep your foot from being caught.

3:27

Do not withhold good from those to whom it is

your foot will not stumble.

3:24

If you sit down, you will not be afraid; when you lie down, your sleep will be sweet.

3:25

Do not be afraid of sudden panic, or of the ruin of the wicked, when it comes;

3:26

for the LORD will be your confidence and will keep your foot from being caught.

3:27

Do not withhold good from those to whom it is

due, when it is in your power to do it.

3:28

Do not say to your neighbor, "Go, and come again, tomorrow I will give it" - when you have it with you.

3:29

Do not plan evil against your neighbor who dwells trustingly beside you.

3:30

Do not contend with a man for no reason, when he has done you no harm.

due, when it is in your power to do it.

3:28

Do not say to your neighbor, “Go, and come again, tomorrow I will give it” - when you have it with you.

3:29

Do not plan evil against your neighbor who dwells trustingly beside you.

3:30

Do not contend with a man for no reason, when he has done you no harm.

3:31
Do not envy a man of violence and do not choose any of his ways;
3:32
for the perverse man is an abomination to the LORD, but the upright are in his confidence.
3:33
The LORD's curse is on the house of the wicked, but he blesses the abode of the righteous.
3:34
Toward the scorners he is scornful, but to the humble he shows favor.

3:31
Do not envy a man of violence and do not choose any of his ways;
3:32
for the perverse man is an abomination to the LORD, but the upright are in his confidence.
3:33
The LORD's curse is on the house of the wicked, but he blesses the abode of the righteous.
3:34
Toward the scorners he is scornful, but to the humble he shows favor.

3:35
The wise will inherit honor, but fools get disgrace.

Proberbs 4

4:1
Hear, O sons, a father's instruction, and be attentive, that you may gain insight;
4:2
for I give you good precepts: do not forsake my teaching.
4:3
When I was a son with my father, tender, the only one in the sight of my mother,

3:35
The wise will inherit honor, but fools get disgrace.

Proberbs 4
4:1
Hear, O sons, a father's instruction, and be attentive, that you may gain insight;
4:2
for I give you good precepts: do not forsake my teaching.

4:3
When I was a son with my father, tender, the only one in the sight of my mother,

4:4
he taught me, and said to me, "Let your heart hold fast my words; keep my commandments, and live;
4:5
do not forget, and do not turn away from the words of my mouth. Get wisdom; get insight.
4:6
Do not forsake her, and she will keep you; love her, and she will guard you.
4:7
The beginning of wisdom is this: Get wisdom, and

4:4
he taught me, and said to me, "Let your heart hold fast my words; keep my commandments, and live;
4:5
do not forget, and do not turn away from the words of my mouth. Get wisdom; get insight.
4:6
Do not forsake her, and she will keep you; love her, and she will guard you.
4:7
The beginning of wisdom is this: Get wisdom, and

whatever you get, get insight.

4:8
Prize her highly, and she will exalt you; she will honor you if you embrace her.

4:9
She will place on your head a fair garland; she will bestow on you a beautiful crown."

4:10
Hear, my son, and accept my words, that the years of your life may be many.

4:11
I have taught you the way

whatever you get, get insight.

4:8
Prize her highly, and she will exalt you; she will honor you if you embrace her.

4:9
She will place on your head a fair garland; she will bestow on you a beautiful crown."

4:10
Hear, my son, and accept my words, that the years of your life may be many.

4:11
I have taught you the way

of wisdom; I have led you
in the paths of uprightness.

4:12
When you walk, your step
will not be hampered; and
if you run, you will not
stumble.

4:13
Keep hold of instruction,
do not let go;
guard her, for she is your
life.

4:14
Do not enter the path of
the wicked, and do not
walk in the way of evil
men.

of wisdom; I have led you in the paths of uprightness.
4:12
When you walk, your step will not be hampered; and if you run, you will not stumble.
4:13
Keep hold of instruction, do not let go; guard her, for she is your life.
4:14
Do not enter the path of the wicked, and do not walk in the way of evil men.

4:15
Avoid it; do not go on it; turn away from it and pass on.

4:16
For they cannot sleep unless they have done wrong; they are robbed of sleep unless they have made some one stumble.

4:17
For they eat the bread of wickedness and drink the wine of violence.

4:18
But the path of the righteous is like the light of dawn, which shines brighter

4:15
Avoid it; do not go on it; turn away from it and pass on.

4:16
For they cannot sleep unless they have done wrong; they are robbed of sleep unless they have made some one stumble.

4:17
For they eat the bread of wickedness and drink the wine of violence.

4:18
But the path of the righteous is like the light of dawn, which shines brighter

and brighter until full day.

4:19

The way of the wicked is like deep darkness; they do not know over what they stumble.

4:20

My son, be attentive to my words; incline your ear to my sayings.

4:21

Let them not escape from your sight; keep them within your heart.

4:22

For they are life to him who finds them, and healing to all his flesh.

and brighter until full day.

4:19

The way of the wicked is like deep darkness; they do not know over what they stumble.

4:20

My son, be attentive to my words; incline your ear to my sayings.

4:21

Let them not escape from your sight; keep them within your heart.

4:22

For they are life to him who finds them, and healing to all his flesh.

4:23
Keep your heart with all vigilance; for from it flow the springs of life.
4:24
Put away from you crooked speech, and put devious talk far from you.
4:25
Let your eyes look directly forward, and your gaze be straight before you.
4:26
Take heed to the path of your feet, then all your ways will be sure.
4:27
Do not swerve to the right

4:23
Keep your heart with all vigilance; for from it flow the springs of life.
4:24
Put away from you crooked speech, and put devious talk far from you.
4:25
Let your eyes look directly forward, and your gaze be straight before you.
4:26
Take heed to the path of your feet, then all your ways will be sure.
4:27
Do not swerve to the right

or to the left; turn your foot away from evil.

Proberbs 5

5:1

My son, be attentive to my wisdom, incline your ear to my understanding;

5:2

that you may keep discretion, and your lips may guard knowledge.

5:3

For the lips of a loose woman drip honey, and her speech is smoother than oil;

or to the left; turn your foot away from evil.

Proberbs 5

5:1

My son, be attentive to my wisdom, incline your ear to my understanding;

5:2

that you may keep discretion, and your lips may guard knowledge.

5:3

For the lips of a loose woman drip honey, and her speech is smoother than oil;

5:4
but in the end she is bitter as wormwood, sharp as a two-edged sword.

5:5
Her feet go down to death; her steps follow the path to Sheol;

5:6
she does not take heed to the path of life; her ways wander, and she does not know it.

5:7
And now, O sons, listen to me, and do not depart from the words of my mouth.

5:4
but in the end she is bitter as wormwood, sharp as a two-edged sword.

5:5
Her feet go down to death; her steps follow the path to Sheol;

5:6
she does not take heed to the path of life; her ways wander, and she does not know it.

5:7
And now, O sons, listen to me, and do not depart from the words of my mouth.

5:8
Keep your way far from her, and do not go near the door of her house;
5:9
lest you give your honor to others and your years to the merciless;
5:10
lest strangers take their fill of your strength, and your labors go to the house of an alien;
5:11
and at the end of your life you groan, when your flesh and body are consumed,

5:8
Keep your way far from her, and do not go near the door of her house;
5:9
lest you give your honor to others and your years to the merciless;
5:10
lest strangers take their fill of your strength, and your labors go to the house of an alien;
5:11
and at the end of your life you groan, when your flesh and body are consumed,

5:12
and you say, "How I hated discipline, and my heart despised reproof!
5:13
I did not listen to the voice of my teachers or incline my ear to my instructors.
5:14
I was at the point of utter ruin in the assembled congregation."
5:15
Drink water from your own cistern, flowing water from your own well.
5:16
Should your springs be

5:12
and you say, "How I hated discipline, and my heart despised reproof!
5:13
I did not listen to the voice of my teachers or incline my ear to my instructors.
5:14
I was at the point of utter ruin in the assembled congregation."
5:15
Drink water from your own cistern, flowing water from your own well.
5:16
Should your springs be

scattered abroad, streams of water in the streets?
5:17
Let them be for yourself alone, and not for strangers with you.
5:18
Let your fountain be blessed, and rejoice in the wife of your youth,
5:19
a lovely hind, a graceful doe. Let her affection fill you at all times with delight, be infatuated always with her love.
5:20
Why should you be

scattered abroad, streams of water in the streets?
5:17
Let them be for yourself alone, and not for strangers with you.
5:18
Let your fountain be blessed, and rejoice in the wife of your youth,
5:19
a lovely hind, a graceful doe. Let her affection fill you at all times with delight, be infatuated always with her love.
5:20
Why should you be

infatuated, my son, with a loose woman and embrace the bosom of an adventuress?

5:21
For a man's ways are before the eyes of the LORD, and he watches all his paths.

5:22
The iniquities of the wicked ensnare him, and he is caught in the toils of his sin.

5:23
He dies for lack of discipline, and because of

infatuated, my son, with a loose woman and embrace the bosom of an adventuress?

5:21
For a man's ways are before the eyes of the LORD, and he watches all his paths.

5:22
The iniquities of the wicked ensnare him, and he is caught in the toils of his sin.

5:23
He dies for lack of discipline, and because of

his great folly he is lost.

Proberbs 6

6:1
My son, if you have become surety for your neighbor, have given your pledge for a stranger;
6:2
if you are snared in the utterance of your lips, caught in the words of your mouth;
6:3
then do this, my son, and save yourself, for you have come into your neighbor's

his great folly he is lost.

Proberbs 6
6:1
My son, if you have become surety for your neighbor, have given your pledge for a stranger;
6:2
if you are snared in the utterance of your lips, caught in the words of your mouth;
6:3
then do this, my son, and save yourself, for you have come into your neighbor's

power: go, hasten, and importune your neighbor.

6:4
Give your eyes no sleep and your eyelids no slumber;

6:5
save yourself like a gazelle from the hunter, like a bird from the hand of the fowler.

6:6
Go to the ant, O sluggard; consider her ways, and be wise.

6:7
Without having any chief, officer or ruler,

power: go, hasten, and importune your neighbor.

6:4
Give your eyes no sleep and your eyelids no slumber;

6:5
save yourself like a gazelle from the hunter, like a bird from the hand of the fowler.

6:6
Go to the ant, O sluggard; consider her ways, and be wise.

6:7
Without having any chief, officer or ruler,

6:8
she prepares her food in summer, and gathers her sustenance in harvest.

6:9
How long will you lie there, O sluggard? When will you arise from your sleep?

6:10
A little sleep, a little slumber, a little folding of the hands to rest,

6:11
and poverty will come upon you like a vagabond, and want like an armed man.

6:8
she prepares her food in summer, and gathers her sustenance in harvest.

6:9
How long will you lie there, O sluggard? When will you arise from your sleep?

6:10
A little sleep, a little slumber, a little folding of the hands to rest,

6:11
and poverty will come upon you like a vagabond, and want like an armed man.

6:12
A worthless person, a wicked man, goes about with crooked speech,
6:13
winks with his eyes, scrapes with his feet, points with his finger,
6:14
with perverted heart devises evil, continually sowing discord;
6:15
therefore calamity will come upon him suddenly; in a moment he will be broken beyond healing.

6:12
A worthless person, a wicked man, goes about with crooked speech,

6:13
winks with his eyes, scrapes with his feet, points with his finger,
6:14
with perverted heart devises evil, continually sowing discord;

6:15
therefore calamity will come upon him suddenly; in a moment he will be broken beyond healing.

6:16
There are six things which the LORD hates, seven which are an abomination to him:

6:17
haughty eyes, a lying tongue, and hands that shed innocent blood,

6:18
a heart that devises wicked plans, feet that make haste to run to evil,

6:19
a false witness who breathes out lies, and a man who sows discord among brothers.

6:16
There are six things which the LORD hates, seven which are an abomination to him:

6:17
haughty eyes, a lying tongue, and hands that shed innocent blood,

6:18
a heart that devises wicked plans, feet that make haste to run to evil,

6:19
a false witness who breathes out lies, and a man who sows discord among brothers.

6:20
My son, keep your father's commandment, and forsake not your mother's teaching.
6:21
Bind them upon your heart always; tie them about your neck.
6:22
When you walk, they will lead you; when you lie down, they will watch over you; and when you awake, they will talk with you.
6:23
For the commandment is a lamp and the teaching a

6:20
My son, keep your father's commandment, and forsake not your mother's teaching.
6:21
Bind them upon your heart always; tie them about your neck.
6:22
When you walk, they will lead you; when you lie down, they will watch over you; and when you awake, they will talk with you.
6:23
For the commandment is a lamp and the teaching a

light, and the reproofs of discipline are the way of life,

6:24

to preserve you from the evil woman, from the smooth tongue of the adventuress.

6:25

Do not desire her beauty in your heart, and do not let her capture you with her eyelashes;

6:26

for a harlot may be hired for a loaf of bread, but an adulteress stalks a man's

light, and the reproofs of discipline are the way of life,

6:24

to preserve you from the evil woman, from the smooth tongue of the adventuress.

6:25

Do not desire her beauty in your heart, and do not let her capture you with her eyelashes;

6:26

for a harlot may be hired for a loaf of bread, but an adulteress stalks a man's very life.

6:27
Can a man carry fire in his bosom and his clothes not be burned?

6:28
Or can one walk upon hot coals and his feet not be scorched?

6:29
So is he who goes in to his neighbor's wife; none who touches her will go unpunished.

6:30
Do not men despise a thief if he steals to satisfy his appetite when he is

very life.
6:27
Can a man carry fire in his bosom and his clothes not be burned?

6:28
Or can one walk upon hot coals and his feet not be scorched?

6:29
So is he who goes in to his neighbor's wife; none who touches her will go unpunished.

6:30
Do not men despise a thief if he steals to satisfy his appetite when he is

hungry?

6:31
And if he is caught, he will pay sevenfold; he will give all the goods of his house.

6:32
He who commits adultery has no sense; he who does it destroys himself.

6:33
Wounds and dishonor will he get, and his disgrace will not be wiped away.

6:34
For jealousy makes a man furious, and he will not spare when he takes

hungry?

6:31
And if he is caught, he will pay sevenfold; he will give all the goods of his house.

6:32
He who commits adultery has no sense; he who does it destroys himself.

6:33
Wounds and dishonor will he get, and his disgrace will not be wiped away.

6:34
For jealousy makes a man furious, and he will not spare when he takes

revenge.

6:35
He will accept no compensation, nor be appeased though you multiply gifts.

Proberbs 7

7:1
My son, keep my words and treasure up my commandments with you;
7:2
keep my commandments and live, keep my teachings as the apple of your eye;
7:3
bind them on your fingers,

revenge.

6:35
He will accept no compensation, nor be appeased though you multiply gifts.

Proberbs 7
7:1
My son, keep my words and treasure up my commandments with you;
7:2
keep my commandments and live, keep my teachings as the apple of your eye;
7:3
bind them on your fingers,

write them on the tablet of
your heart.
7:4
Say to wisdom, "You are
my sister," and call insight
your intimate friend;
7:5
to preserve you from the
loose woman, from the
adventuress with her smooth
words.
7:6
For at the window of my
house I have looked out
through my lattice,
7:7
and I have seen among the
simple, I have perceived

write them on
the tablet of
your heart.
7:4
Say to
wisdom, "You
are my
sister," and
call insight
your intimate
friend;
7:5
to preserve
you from the
loose woman,
from the
adventuress
with her
smooth words.
7:6
For at the
window of my
house I have
looked out
through my
lattice,
7:7
and I have
seen among
the simple, I
have
perceived

among the youths, a young man without sense,

7:8

passing along the street near her corner, taking the road to her house

7:9

in the twilight, in the evening, at the time of night and darkness.

7:10

And lo, a woman meets him, dressed as a harlot, wily of heart.

7:11

She is loud and wayward, her feet do not stay at home;

among the youths, a young man without sense,

7:8

passing along the street near her corner, taking the road to her house

7:9

in the twilight, in the evening, at the time of night and darkness.

7:10

And lo, a woman meets him, dressed as a harlot, wily of heart.

7:11

She is loud and wayward, her feet do not stay at home;

7:12
now in the street, now in the market, and at every corner she lies in wait.

7:13
She seizes him and kisses him, and with impudent face she says to him:

7:14
"I had to offer sacrifices, and today I have paid my vows;

7:15
so now I have come out to meet you, to seek you eagerly, and I have found you.

7:12
now in the street, now in the market, and at every corner she lies in wait.
7:13
She seizes him and kisses him, and with impudent face she says to him:
7:14
"I had to offer sacrifices, and today I have paid my vows;
7:15
so now I have come out to meet you, to seek you eagerly, and I have found you.

7:16
I have decked my couch with coverings, colored spreads of Egyptian linen;
7:17
I have perfumed my bed with myrrh, aloes, and cinnamon.
7:18
Come, let us take our fill of love till morning; let us delight ourselves
with love.
7:19
For my husband is not at home; he has gone on a long journey;

7:16
I have decked my couch with coverings, colored spreads of Egyptian linen;
7:17
I have perfumed my bed with myrrh, aloes, and cinnamon.
7:18
Come, let us take our fill of love till morning; let us delight ourselves with love.
7:19
For my husband is not at home; he has gone on a long journey;

7:20
he took a bag of money with him; at full moon he will come home."

7:21
With much seductive speech she persuades him; with her smooth talk she compels him.

7:22
All at once he follows her, as an ox goes to the slaughter, or as a stag is caught fast

7:23
till an arrow pierces its entrails; as a bird rushes into a snare; he does not

7:20
he took a bag of money with him; at full moon he will come home."

7:21
With much seductive speech she persuades him; with her smooth talk she compels him.

7:22
All at once he follows her, as an ox goes to the slaughter, or as a stag is caught fast

7:23
till an arrow pierces its entrails; as a bird rushes into a snare; he does not

know that it will cost him
his life.

7:24

And now, O sons, listen to
me, and be attentive to the
words of my mouth.

7:25

Let not your heart turn
aside to her ways, do not
stray into her paths;

7:26

for many a victim has she
laid low; yea, all her slain
are a mighty host.

7:27

Her house is the way to
Sheol, going down to the
chambers of death.

know that it
will cost him
his life.

7:24

And now, O
sons, listen to
me, and be
attentive to
the words of
my mouth.

7:25

Let not your
heart turn
aside to her
ways, do not
stray into her
paths;

7:26

for many a
victim has
she laid low;
yea, all her
slain are a
mighty host.

7:27

Her house is
the way to
Sheol, going
down to the
chambers of
death.

Proberbs 8

8:1
Does not wisdom call, does not understanding raise her voice?
8:2
On the heights beside the way, in the paths she takes her stand;
8:3
beside the gates in front of the town, at the entrance of the portals she cries aloud:
8:4
"To you, O men, I call, and my cry is to the sons of men.

Proberbs 8
8:1
Does not wisdom call, does not understanding raise her voice?
8:2
On the heights beside the way, in the paths she takes her stand;
8:3
beside the gates in front of the town, at the entrance of the portals she cries aloud:
8:4
"To you, O men, I call, and my cry is to the sons of men.

8:5
O simple ones, learn prudence; O foolish men, pay attention.

8:6
Hear, for I will speak noble things, and from my lips will come what is right;

8:7
for my mouth will utter truth; wickedness is an abomination to my lips.

8:8
All the words of my mouth are righteous; there is nothing twisted or crooked in them.

8:5
O simple ones, learn prudence; O foolish men, pay attention.

8:6
Hear, for I will speak noble things, and from my lips will come what is right;

8:7
for my mouth will utter truth; wickedness is an abomination to my lips.

8:8
All the words of my mouth are righteous; there is nothing twisted or crooked in them.

8:9

They are all straight to him who understands and right to those who find knowledge.

8:10

Take my instruction instead of silver, and knowledge rather than choice gold;

8:11

for wisdom is better than jewels, and all that you may desire cannot compare with her.

8:12

I, wisdom, dwell in prudence, and I find knowledge and

8:9

They are all straight to him who understands and right to those who find knowledge.

8:10

Take my instruction instead of silver, and knowledge rather than choice gold;

8:11

for wisdom is better than jewels, and all that you may desire cannot compare with her.

8:12

I, wisdom, dwell in prudence, and I find knowledge and

discretion.

8:13

The fear of the LORD is hatred of evil. Pride and arrogance and the way of evil and perverted speech I hate.

8:14

I have counsel and sound wisdom, I have insight, I have strength.

8:15

By me kings reign, and rulers decree what is just;

8:16

by me princes rule, and nobles govern the earth.

discretion.

8:13

The fear of the LORD is hatred of evil. Pride and arrogance and the way of evil and perverted speech I hate.

8:14

I have counsel and sound wisdom, I have insight, I have strength.

8:15

By me kings reign, and rulers decree what is just;

8:16

by me princes rule, and nobles govern the earth.

8:17
I love those who love me, and those who seek me diligently find me.

8:18
Riches and honor are with me, enduring wealth and prosperity.

8:19
My fruit is better than gold, even fine gold, and my yield than choice silver.

8:20
I walk in the way of righteousness, in the paths of justice,

8:21
endowing with wealth those

8:17
I love those who love me, and those who seek me diligently find me.

8:18
Riches and honor are with me, enduring wealth and prosperity.

8:19
My fruit is better than gold, even fine gold, and my yield than choice silver.

8:20
I walk in the way of righteousness, in the paths of justice,

8:21
endowing with wealth those

who love me, and filling
their treasuries.
8:22
The LORD created me at
the beginning of his work,
the first of his acts of old.
8:23
Ages ago I was set up, at
the first, before the
beginning of the earth.
8:24
When there were no depths
I was brought forth, when
there were no springs
abounding with water.
8:25
Before the mountains

who love me, and filling their treasuries.
8:22
The LORD created me at the beginning of his work, the first of his acts of old.
8:23
Ages ago I was set up, at the first, before the beginning of the earth.
8:24
When there were no depths I was brought forth, when there were no springs abounding with water.
8:25
Before the mountains

had been shaped, before the hills, I was brought forth;

8:26

before he had made the earth with its fields, or the first of the dust of the world.

8:27

When he established the heavens, I was there, when he drew a circle on the face of the deep,

8:28

when he made firm the skies above, when he established the fountains of the deep,

had been shaped, before the hills, I was brought forth;

8:26

before he had made the earth with its fields, or the first of the dust of the world.

8:27

When he established the heavens, I was there, when he drew a circle on the face of the deep,

8:28

when he made firm the skies above, when he established the fountains of the deep,

8:29
when he assigned to the sea its limit, so that the waters might not transgress his command, when he marked out the foundations of the earth,

8:30
then I was beside him, like a master workman; and I was daily his delight, rejoicing before him always,

8:31
rejoicing in his inhabited world and delighting in the sons of men.

8:29
when he assigned to the sea its limit, so that the waters might not transgress his command, when he marked out the foundations of the earth,

8:30
then I was beside him, like a master workman; and I was daily his delight, rejoicing before him always,

8:31
rejoicing in his inhabited world and delighting in the sons of men.

8:32
And now, my sons, listen to me: happy are those who keep my ways.
8:33
Hear instruction and be wise, and do not neglect it.
8:34
Happy is the man who listens to me, watching daily at my gates, waiting beside my doors.
8:35
For he who finds me finds life and obtains favor from the LORD;
8:36
but he who misses me

8:32
And now, my sons, listen to me: happy are those who keep my ways.
8:33
Hear instruction and be wise, and do not neglect it.
8:34
Happy is the man who listens to me, watching daily at my gates, waiting beside my doors.
8:35
For he who finds me finds life and obtains favor from the LORD;
8:36
but he who misses me

injures himself; all who
hate me love death."

Proberbs 9

9:1
Wisdom has built her
house, she has set up her
seven pillars.
9:2
She has slaughtered her
beasts, she has mixed her
wine, she has also set her
table.
9:3
She has sent out her
maids to call from the
highest places in the town,

injures
himself; all
who hate me
love death."

Proberbs 9
9:1
Wisdom has
built her
house, she
has set up
her seven
pillars.
9:2
She has
slaughtered
her beasts,
she has mixed
her wine, she
has also set
her table.

9:3
She has sent
out her maids
to call from
the highest
places in the
town,

9:4
"Whoever is simple, let him turn in here!" To him who is without sense she says,
9:5
"Come, eat of my bread and drink of the wine I have mixed.
9:6
Leave simpleness, and live, and walk in the way of insight."
9:7
He who corrects a scoffer gets himself abuse, and he who reproves a wicked man incurs injury.

9:4
"Whoever is simple, let him turn in here!" To him who is without sense she says,
9:5
"Come, eat of my bread and drink of the wine I have mixed.
9:6
Leave simpleness, and live, and walk in the way of insight."
9:7
He who corrects a scoffer gets himself abuse, and he who reproves a wicked man incurs injury.

9:8
Do not reprove a scoffer,
or he will hate you;
reprove a wise man, and
he will love you.
9:9
Give instruction to a wise
man, and he will be still
wiser; teach a righteous
man and he will increase
in learning.
9:10
The fear of the LORD is
the beginning of wisdom,
and the knowledge of the
Holy One is insight.
9:11
For by me your days will

9:8
Do not reprove a scoffer, or he will hate you; reprove a wise man, and he will love you.
9:9
Give instruction to a wise man, and he will be still wiser; teach a righteous man and he will increase in learning.
9:10
The fear of the LORD is the beginning of wisdom, and the knowledge of the Holy One is insight.
9:11
For by me your days will

be multiplied, and years will be added to your life.

9:12
If you are wise, you are wise for yourself; if you scoff, you alone will bear it.

9:13
A foolish woman is noisy; she is wanton and knows no shame.

9:14
She sits at the door of her house, she takes a seat on the high places of the town,

9:15
calling to those who pass by, who are going

be multiplied, and years will be added to your life.

9:12
If you are wise, you are wise for yourself; if you scoff, you alone will bear it.

9:13
A foolish woman is noisy; she is wanton and knows no shame.

9:14
She sits at the door of her house, she takes a seat on the high places of the town,

9:15
calling to those who pass by, who are going

straight on their way,
9:16
"Whoever is simple, let him turn in here!" And to him who is without sense she says,
9:17
"Stolen water is sweet, and bread eaten in secret is pleasant."
9:18
But he does not know that the dead are there, that her guests are in the depths of Sheol.

straight on their way.
9:16
"Whoever is simple, let him turn in here!" And to him who is without sense she says,
9:17
"Stolen water is sweet, and bread eaten in secret is pleasant."
9:18
But he does not know that the dead are there, that her guests are in the depths of Sheol.

Proberbs 10

10:1
The proverbs of Solomon.
A wise son makes a glad
father, but a foolish son is
a sorrow to his mother.

10:2
Treasures gained by
wickedness do not profit,
but righteousness delivers
from death.

10:3
The LORD does not let the
righteous go hungry, but he
thwarts the craving of the
wicked.

10:4
A slack hand causes

Proberbs 10
10:1
The proverbs
of Solomon. A
wise son
makes a glad
father, but a
foolish son is
a sorrow to
his mother.

10:2
Treasures
gained by
wickedness do
not profit, but
righteousness
delivers from
death.

10:3
The LORD
does not let
the righteous
go hungry,
but he
thwarts the
craving of the
wicked.
10:4
A slack hand
causes

poverty, but the hand of the diligent makes rich.

10:5

A son who gathers in summer is prudent, but a son who sleeps in harvest brings shame.

10:6

Blessings are on the head of the righteous, but the mouth of the wicked conceals violence.

10:7

The memory of the righteous is a blessing, but the name of the wicked will rot.

poverty, but the hand of the diligent makes rich.

10:5

A son who gathers in summer is prudent, but a son who sleeps in harvest brings shame.

10:6

Blessings are on the head of the righteous, but the mouth of the wicked conceals violence.

10:7

The memory of the righteous is a blessing, but the name of the wicked will rot.

10:8
The wise of heart will heed commandments, but a prating fool will come to ruin.

10:9
He who walks in integrity walks securely, but he who perverts his ways will be found out.

10:10
He who winks the eye causes trouble, but he who boldly reproves makes peace.

10:11
The mouth of the righteous is a fountain of life, but

10:8
The wise of heart will heed commandments, but a prating fool will come to ruin.

10:9
He who walks in integrity walks securely, but he who perverts his ways will be found out.

10:10
He who winks the eye causes trouble, but he who boldly reproves makes peace.

10:11
The mouth of the righteous is a fountain of life, but

the mouth of the wicked conceals violence.

10:12

Hatred stirs up strife, but love covers all offenses.

10:13

On the lips of him who has understanding wisdom is found, but a rod is for the back of him who lacks sense.

10:14

Wise men lay up knowledge, but the babbling of a fool brings ruin near.

10:15

A rich man's wealth is his strong city; the poverty of

the mouth of the wicked conceals violence.

10:12

Hatred stirs up strife, but love covers all offenses.

10:13

On the lips of him who has understanding wisdom is found, but a rod is for the back of him who lacks sense.

10:14

Wise men lay up knowledge, but the babbling of a fool brings ruin near.

10:15

A rich man's wealth is his strong city; the poverty of

the poor is their ruin.

10:16
The wage of the righteous leads to life, the gain of the wicked to sin.

10:17
He who heeds instruction is on the path to life, but he who rejects reproof goes astray.

10:18
He who conceals hatred has lying lips, and he who utters slander is a fool.

10:19
When words are many, transgression is not lacking, but he who restrains his

the poor is their ruin.

10:16
The wage of the righteous leads to life, the gain of the wicked to sin.

10:17
He who heeds instruction is on the path to life, but he who rejects reproof goes astray.

10:18
He who conceals hatred has lying lips, and he who utters slander is a fool.

10:19
When words are many, transgression is not lacking, but he who restrains his

lips is prudent.

10:20
The tongue of the righteous is choice silver; the mind of the wicked is of little worth.

10:21
The lips of the righteous feed many, but fools die for lack of sense.

10:22
The blessing of the LORD makes rich, and he adds no sorrow with it.

10:23
It is like sport to a fool to do wrong, but wise conduct is pleasure to a man of

lips is prudent.

10:20
The tongue of the righteous is choice silver; the mind of the wicked is of little worth.

10:21
The lips of the righteous feed many, but fools die for lack of sense.

10:22
The blessing of the LORD makes rich, and he adds no sorrow with it.

10:23
It is like sport to a fool to do wrong, but wise conduct is pleasure to a man of

understanding.
10:24
What the wicked dreads will come upon him, but the desire of the righteous will be granted.
10:25
When the tempest passes, the wicked is no more, but the righteous is established for ever.
10:26
Like vinegar to the teeth, and smoke to the eyes, so is the sluggard to those who send him.
10:27
The fear of the LORD

understanding.
10:24
What the wicked dreads will come upon him, but the desire of the righteous will be granted.
10:25
When the tempest passes, the wicked is no more, but the righteous is established for ever.
10:26
Like vinegar to the teeth, and smoke to the eyes, so is the sluggard to those who send him.
10:27
The fear of the LORD

prolongs life, but the years of the wicked will be short.

10:28
The hope of the righteous ends in gladness, but the expectation of the wicked comes to nought.

10:29
The LORD is a stronghold to him whose way is upright, but destruction to evildoers.

10:30
The righteous will never be removed, but the wicked will not dwell in the land.

10:31
The mouth of the righteous

prolongs life, but the years of the wicked will be short.
10:28
The hope of the righteous ends in gladness, but the expectation of the wicked comes to nought.
10:29
The LORD is a stronghold to him whose way is upright, but destruction to evildoers.
10:30
The righteous will never be removed, but the wicked will not dwell in the land.
10:31
The mouth of the righteous

brings forth wisdom, but the perverse tongue will be cut off.

10:32
The lips of the righteous know what is acceptable, but the mouth of the wicked, what is perverse.

Proberbs 11

11:1
A false balance is an abomination to the LORD, but a just weight is his delight.

11:2
When pride comes, then

brings forth wisdom, but the perverse tongue will be cut off.

10:32
The lips of the righteous know what is acceptable, but the mouth of the wicked, what is perverse.

Proberbs 11
11:1
A false balance is an abomination to the LORD, but a just weight is his delight.

11:2
When pride comes, then

comes disgrace; but with the humble is wisdom.

11:3

The integrity of the upright guides them, but the crookedness of the treacherous destroys them.

11:4

Riches do not profit in the day of wrath, but righteousness delivers from death.

11:5

The righteousness of the blameless keeps his way straight, but the wicked falls by his

comes disgrace; but with the humble is wisdom.

11:3

The integrity of the upright guides them, but the crookedness of the treacherous destroys them.

11:4

Riches do not profit in the day of wrath, but righteousness delivers from death.

11:5

The righteousness of the blameless keeps his way straight, but the wicked falls by his *own wickedness.*

11:6

The righteousness of the upright delivers them, but the treacherous are taken captive by their lust.

11:7

When the wicked dies, his hope perishes, and the expectation of the godless comes to nought.

11:8

The righteous is delivered from trouble, and the wicked gets into it instead.

11:9

With his mouth the

own
wickedness.
11:6
The
righteousness
of the upright
delivers them,
but the
treacherous
are taken
captive by
their lust.
11:7
When the
wicked dies,
his hope
perishes, and
the
expectation of
the godless
comes to
nought.
11:8
The righteous
is delivered
from trouble,
and the
wicked gets
into it instead.
11:9
With his
mouth the

godless man would destroy his neighbor, but by knowledge the righteous are delivered.

11:10
When it goes well with the righteous, the city rejoices; and when the wicked perish there are shouts of gladness.

11:11
By the blessing of the upright a city is exalted, but it is overthrown by the mouth of the wicked.

11:12
He who belittles his

godless man would destroy his neighbor, but by knowledge the righteous are delivered.

11:10
When it goes well with the righteous, the city rejoices; and when the wicked perish there are shouts of gladness.

11:11
By the blessing of the upright a city is exalted, but it is overthrown by the mouth of the wicked.
11:12
He who belittles his

neighbor lacks sense, but a man of understanding remains silent.

11:13

He who goes about as a talebearer reveals secrets, but he who is trustworthy in spirit keeps a thing hidden.

11:14

Where there is no guidance, a people falls; but in an abundance of counselors there is safety.

11:15

He who gives surety for a stranger will smart for it,

neighbor lacks sense, but a man of understanding remains silent.

11:13

He who goes about as a talebearer reveals secrets, but he who is trustworthy in spirit keeps a thing hidden.

11:14

Where there is no guidance, a people falls; but in an abundance of counselors there is safety.

11:15

He who gives surety for a stranger will smart for it.

but he who hates suretyship is secure.

11:16

A gracious woman gets honor, and violent men get riches.

11:17

A man who is kind benefits himself, but a cruel man hurts himself.

11:18

A wicked man earns deceptive wages, but one who sows righteousness gets a sure reward.

11:19

He who is steadfast in righteousness will live, but

but he who hates suretyship is secure.

11:16

A gracious woman gets honor, and violent men get riches.

11:17

A man who is kind benefits himself, but a cruel man hurts himself.

11:18

A wicked man earns deceptive wages, but one who sows righteousness gets a sure reward.

11:19

He who is steadfast in righteousness will live, but

he who pursues evil will die.

11:20

Men of perverse mind are an abomination to the LORD, but those of blameless ways are his delight.

11:21

Be assured, an evil man will not go unpunished, but those who are righteous will be delivered.

11:22

Like a gold ring in a swine's snout is a beautiful woman without discretion.

he who pursues evil will die.

11:20

Men of perverse mind are an abomination to the LORD, but those of blameless ways are his delight.

11:21

Be assured, an evil man will not go unpunished, but those who are righteous will be delivered.

11:22

Like a gold ring in a swine's snout is a beautiful woman without discretion.

11:23
The desire of the righteous ends only in good; the expectation of the wicked in wrath.

11:24
One man gives freely, yet grows all the richer; another withholds what he should give, and only suffers want.

11:25
A liberal man will be enriched, and one who waters will himself be watered.

11:26
The people curse him who

11:23
The desire of the righteous ends only in good; the expectation of the wicked in wrath.

11:24
One man gives freely, yet grows all the richer; another withholds what he should give, and only suffers want.

11:25
A liberal man will be enriched, and one who waters will himself be watered.

11:26
The people curse him who

holds back grain, but a blessing is on the head of him who sells it.

11:27

He who diligently seeks good seeks favor, but evil comes to him who searches for it.

11:28

He who trusts in his riches will wither, but the righteous will flourish like a green leaf.

11:29

He who troubles his household will inherit wind, and the fool will be

holds back grain, but a blessing is on the head of him who sells it.

11:27

He who diligently seeks good seeks favor, but evil comes to him who searches for it.

11:28

He who trusts in his riches will wither, but the righteous will flourish like a green leaf.

11:29

He who troubles his household will inherit wind, and the fool will be *servant to the wise.*

11:30

The fruit of the righteous is a tree of life, but lawlessness takes away lives.

11:31

If the righteous is requited on earth, how much more the wicked and the sinner!

Proberbs 12

12:1

Whoever loves discipline loves knowledge, but he who hates reproof is stupid.

servant to the wise.

11:30

The fruit of the righteous is a tree of life, but lawlessness takes away lives.

11:31

If the righteous is requited on earth, how much more the wicked and the sinner!

Proberbs 12

12:1

Whoever loves discipline loves knowledge, but he who hates reproof is stupid.

12:2
A good man obtains favor from the LORD, but a man of evil devices he condemns.

12:3
A man is not established by wickedness, but the root of the righteous will never be moved.

12:4
A good wife is the crown of her husband, but she who brings shame is like rottenness in his bones.

12:5
The thoughts of the righteous are just; the counsels of

12:2
A good man obtains favor from the LORD, but a man of evil devices he condemns.

12:3
A man is not established by wickedness, but the root of the righteous will never be moved.

12:4
A good wife is the crown of her husband, but she who brings shame is like rottenness in his bones.

12:5
The thoughts of the righteous are just; the counsels of the wicked

the wicked are treacherous.

12:6

The words of the wicked lie in wait for blood, but the mouth of the upright delivers men.

12:7

The wicked are overthrown and are no more, but the house of the righteous will stand.

12:8

A man is commended according to his good sense, but one of perverse mind is despised.

12:9

Better is a man of

are treacherous.

12:6

The words of the wicked lie in wait for blood, but the mouth of the upright delivers men.

12:7

The wicked are overthrown and are no more, but the house of the righteous will stand.

12:8

A man is commended according to his good sense, but one of perverse mind is despised.

12:9

Better is a man of

humble standing who works for himself than one who plays the great man but lacks bread.

12:10

A righteous man has regard for the life of his beast, but the mercy of the wicked is cruel.

12:11

He who tills his land will have plenty of bread, but he who follows worthless pursuits has no sense.

12:12

The strong tower of the wicked comes to ruin, but

humble standing who works for himself than one who plays the great man but lacks bread.

12:10

A righteous man has regard for the life of his beast, but the mercy of the wicked is cruel.

12:11

He who tills his land will have plenty of bread, but he who follows worthless pursuits has no sense.

12:12

The strong tower of the wicked comes to ruin, but

the root of the righteous stands firm.

12:13
An evil man is ensnared by the transgression of his lips, but the righteous escapes from trouble.

12:14
From the fruit of his words a man is satisfied with good, and the work of a man's hand comes back to him.

12:15
The way of a fool is right in his own eyes, but a wise man listens to advice.

the root of the righteous stands firm.

12:13
An evil man is ensnared by the transgression of his lips, but the righteous escapes from trouble.

12:14
From the fruit of his words a man is satisfied with good, and the work of a man's hand comes back to him.

12:15
The way of a fool is right in his own eyes, but a wise man listens to advice.

12:16
The vexation of a fool is known at once, but the prudent man ignores an insult.

12:17
He who speaks the truth gives honest evidence, but a false witness utters deceit.

12:18
There is one whose rash words are like sword thrusts, but the tongue of the wise brings healing.

12:19
Truthful lips endure for ever, but a lying tongue is but for a

12:16
The vexation of a fool is known at once, but the prudent man ignores an insult.

12:17
He who speaks the truth gives honest evidence, but a false witness utters deceit.

12:18
There is one whose rash words are like sword thrusts, but the tongue of the wise brings healing.

12:19
Truthful lips endure for ever, but a lying tongue is but for a

moment.
12:20
Deceit is in the heart of those who devise evil, but those who plan good have joy.
12:21
No ill befalls the righteous, but the wicked are filled with trouble.
12:22
Lying lips are an abomination to the LORD, but those who act faithfully are his delight.
12:23
A prudent man conceals his knowledge, but fools

moment.
12:20
Deceit is in the heart of those who devise evil, but those who plan good have joy.
12:21
No ill befalls the righteous, but the wicked are filled with trouble.
12:22
Lying lips are an abomination to the LORD, but those who act faithfully are his delight.
12:23
A prudent man conceals his knowledge, but fools

proclaim their folly.

12:24
The hand of the diligent will rule, while the slothful will be put to forced labor.

12:25
Anxiety in a man's heart weighs him down, but a good word makes him glad.

12:26
A righteous man turns away from evil, but the way of the wicked leads them astray.

12:27
A slothful man will not catch his prey, but the diligent man

proclaim their folly.

12:24
The hand of the diligent will rule, while the slothful will be put to forced labor.

12:25
Anxiety in a man's heart weighs him down, but a good word makes him glad.

12:26
A righteous man turns away from evil, but the way of the wicked leads them astray.

12:27
A slothful man will not catch his prey, but the diligent man will get

will get precious wealth.

12:28

In the path of righteousness is life, but the way of error leads to death.

Proberbs 13

13:1

A wise son hears his father's instruction, but a scoffer does not listen to rebuke.

13:2

From the fruit of his mouth a good man eats good, but the desire of the treacherous is for violence.

precious wealth.

12:28

In the path of righteousness is life, but the way of error leads to death.

Proberbs 13

13:1

A wise son hears his father's instruction, but a scoffer does not listen to rebuke.

13:2

From the fruit of his mouth a good man eats good, but the desire of the treacherous is for violence.

13:3
He who guards his mouth preserves his life; he who opens wide his lips comes to ruin.

13:4
The soul of the sluggard craves, and gets nothing, while the soul of the diligent is richly supplied.

13:5
A righteous man hates falsehood, but a wicked man acts shamefully and disgracefully.

13:6
Righteousness guards him whose way is upright, but

13:3
He who guards his mouth preserves his life; he who opens wide his lips comes to ruin.

13:4
The soul of the sluggard craves, and gets nothing, while the soul of the diligent is richly supplied.

13:5
A righteous man hates falsehood, but a wicked man acts shamefully and disgracefully.

13:6
Righteousness guards him whose way is upright, but

sin overthrows the wicked.

13:7

One man pretends to be rich, yet has nothing; another pretends to be poor, yet has great wealth.

13:8

The ransom of a man's life is his wealth, but a poor man has no means of redemption.

13:9

The light of the righteous rejoices, but the lamp of the wicked will be put out.

13:10

By insolence the heedless

sin overthrows the wicked.

13:7

One man pretends to be rich, yet has nothing; another pretends to be poor, yet has great wealth.

13:8

The ransom of a man's life is his wealth, but a poor man has no means of redemption.

13:9

The light of the righteous rejoices, but the lamp of the wicked will be put out.

13:10

By insolence the heedless
make strife,

make strife, but with those who take advice is wisdom.

13:11
Wealth hastily gotten will dwindle, but he who gathers little by little will increase it.

13:12
Hope deferred makes the heart sick, but a desire fulfilled is a tree of life.

13:13
He who despises the word brings destruction on himself, but he who respects the commandment will be rewarded.

but with those who take advice is wisdom.

13:11
Wealth hastily gotten will dwindle, but he who gathers little by little will increase it.

13:12
Hope deferred makes the heart sick, but a desire fulfilled is a tree of life.

13:13
He who despises the word brings destruction on himself, but he who respects the commandment will be rewarded.

13:14
The teaching of the wise is a fountain of life, that one may avoid the snares of death.

13:15
Good sense wins favor, but the way of the faithless is their ruin.

13:16
In everything a prudent man acts with knowledge, but a fool flaunts his folly.

13:17
A bad messenger plunges men into trouble, but a faithful envoy brings healing.

13:14
The teaching of the wise is a fountain of life, that one may avoid the snares of death.

13:15
Good sense wins favor, but the way of the faithless is their ruin.

13:16
In everything a prudent man acts with knowledge, but a fool flaunts his folly.

13:17
A bad messenger plunges men into trouble, but a faithful envoy brings healing.

13:18
Poverty and disgrace come to him who ignores instruction, but he who heeds reproof is honored.
13:19
A desire fulfilled is sweet to the soul; but to turn away from evil is an abomination to fools.
13:20
He who walks with wise men becomes wise, but the companion of fools will suffer harm.
13:21
Misfortune pursues sinners, but prosperity

13:18
Poverty and disgrace come to him who ignores instruction, but he who heeds reproof is honored.
13:19
A desire fulfilled is sweet to the soul; but to turn away from evil is an abomination to fools.
13:20
He who walks with wise men becomes wise, but the companion of fools will suffer harm.
13:21
Misfortune pursues sinners, but prosperity

rewards the righteous.

13:22

A good man leaves an inheritance to his children's children, but the sinner's wealth is laid up for the righteous.

13:23

The fallow ground of the poor yields much food, but it is swept away through injustice.

13:24

He who spares the rod hates his son, but he who loves him is diligent to discipline him.

rewards the righteous.

13:22

A good man leaves an inheritance to his children's children, but the sinner's wealth is laid up for the righteous.

13:23

The fallow ground of the poor yields much food, but it is swept away through injustice.

13:24

He who spares the rod hates his son, but he who loves him is diligent to discipline him.

13:25
The righteous has enough to satisfy his appetite, but the belly of the wicked suffers want.

Proberbs 14
14:1
Wisdom builds her house, but folly with her own hands tears it down.
14:2
He who walks in uprightness fears the LORD, but he who is devious in his ways despises him.

13:25
The righteous has enough to satisfy his appetite, but the belly of the wicked suffers want.

Proberbs 14
14:1
Wisdom builds her house, but folly with her own hands tears it down.

14:2
He who walks in uprightness fears the LORD, but he who is devious in his ways despises him.

14:3
The talk of a fool is a rod for his back, but the lips of the wise will preserve them.

14:4
Where there are no oxen, there is no grain; but abundant crops come by the strength of the ox.

14:5
A faithful witness does not lie, but a false witness breathes out lies.

14:6
A scoffer seeks wisdom in vain, but knowledge is easy for a man of

14:3
The talk of a fool is a rod for his back, but the lips of the wise will preserve them.

14:4
Where there are no oxen, there is no grain; but abundant crops come by the strength of the ox.

14:5
A faithful witness does not lie, but a false witness breathes out lies.

14:6
A scoffer seeks wisdom in vain, but knowledge is easy for a man of

understanding.

14:7

Leave the presence of a fool, for there you do not meet words of knowledge.

14:8

The wisdom of a prudent man is to discern his way, but the folly of fools is deceiving.

14:9

God scorns the wicked, but the upright enjoy his favor.

14:10

The heart knows its own bitterness, and no stranger shares its joy.

understanding.

14:7

Leave the presence of a fool, for there you do not meet words of knowledge.

14:8

The wisdom of a prudent man is to discern his way, but the folly of fools is deceiving.

14:9

God scorns the wicked, but the upright enjoy his favor.

14:10

The heart knows its own bitterness, and no stranger shares its joy.

14:11
The house of the wicked will be destroyed, but the tent of the upright will flourish.

14:12
There is a way which seems right to a man, but its end is the way to death.

14:13
Even in laughter the heart is sad, and the end of joy is grief.

14:14
A perverse man will be filled with the fruit of his ways, and a good man

14:11
The house of the wicked will be destroyed, but the tent of the upright will flourish.

14:12
There is a way which seems right to a man, but its end is the way to death.

14:13
Even in laughter the heart is sad, and the end of joy is grief.

14:14
A perverse man will be filled with the fruit of his ways, and a good man

with the fruit of his deeds.

14:15
The simple believes everything, but the prudent looks where he is going.

14:16
A wise man is cautious and turns away from evil, but a fool throws off restraint and is careless.

14:17
A man of quick temper acts foolishly, but a man of discretion is patient.

14:18
The simple acquire folly, but the prudent are crowned with

with the fruit of his deeds.
14:15
The simple believes everything, but the prudent looks where he is going.
14:16
A wise man is cautious and turns away from evil, but a fool throws off restraint and is careless.
14:17
A man of quick temper acts foolishly, but a man of discretion is patient.
14:18
The simple acquire folly, but the prudent are crowned with

knowledge.

14:19

The evil bow down before the good, the wicked at the gates of the righteous.

14:20

The poor is disliked even by his neighbor, but the rich has many friends.

14:21

He who despises his neighbor is a sinner, but happy is he who is kind to the poor.

14:22

Do they not err that devise evil? Those who devise good meet loyalty and

knowledge.

14:19

The evil bow down before the good, the wicked at the gates of the righteous.

14:20

The poor is disliked even by his neighbor, but the rich has many friends.

14:21

He who despises his neighbor is a sinner, but happy is he who is kind to the poor.

14:22

Do they not err that devise evil? Those who devise good meet loyalty and *faithfulness.*

14:23

In all toil there is profit, but mere talk tends only to want.

14:24

The crown of the wise is their wisdom, but folly is the garland of fools.

14:25

A truthful witness saves lives, but one who utters lies is a betrayer.

14:26

In the fear of the LORD one has strong confidence, and his children will have a refuge.

faithfulness.

14:23
In all toil there is profit, but mere talk tends only to want.

14:24
The crown of the wise is their wisdom, but folly is the garland of fools.

14:25
A truthful witness saves lives, but one who utters lies is a betrayer.

14:26
In the fear of the LORD one has strong confidence, and his children will have a refuge.

14:27
The fear of the LORD is a fountain of life, that one may avoid the snares of death.

14:28
In a multitude of people is the glory of a king, but without people a prince is ruined.

14:29
He who is slow to anger has great understanding, but he who has a hasty temper exalts folly.

14:30
A tranquil mind gives life to the flesh, but passion

14:27
The fear of the LORD is a fountain of life, that one may avoid the snares of death.

14:28
In a multitude of people is the glory of a king, but without people a prince is ruined.

14:29
He who is slow to anger has great understanding, but he who has a hasty temper exalts folly.

14:30
A tranquil mind gives life to the flesh, but passion

makes the bones rot.

14:31

He who oppresses a poor man insults his Maker, but he who is kind to the needy honors him.

14:32

The wicked is overthrown through his evil-doing, but the righteous finds refuge through his integrity.

14:33

Wisdom abides in the mind of a man of understanding, but it is not known in the heart of fools.

14:34

Righteousness exalts a

makes the bones rot.

14:31

He who oppresses a poor man insults his Maker, but he who is kind to the needy honors him.

14:32

The wicked is overthrown through his evil-doing, but the righteous finds refuge through his integrity.

14:33

Wisdom abides in the mind of a man of understanding, but it is not known in the heart of fools.

14:34

Righteousness exalts a

nation, but sin is a
reproach to any people.

14:35
A servant who deals wisely
has the king's favor, but
his wrath falls on one who
acts shamefully.

Proberbs 15

15:1
A soft answer turns away
wrath, but a harsh word
stirs up anger.

15:2
The tongue of the wise
dispenses knowledge, but
the mouths of

nation, but
sin is a
reproach to
any people.
14:35
A servant who
deals wisely
has the king's
favor, but his
wrath falls on
one who acts
shamefully.

Proberbs 15
15:1
A soft answer
turns away
wrath, but a
harsh word
stirs up
anger.
15:2
The tongue of
the wise
dispenses
knowledge,
but the
mouths of

fools pour out folly.
15:3
The eyes of the LORD are in every place, keeping watch on the evil and the good.
15:4
A gentle tongue is a tree of life, but perverseness in it breaks the spirit.
15:5
A fool despises his father's instruction, but he who heeds admonition is prudent.
15:6
In the house of the righteous there is much

fools pour out folly.
15:3
The eyes of the LORD are in every place, keeping watch on the evil and the good.
15:4
A gentle tongue is a tree of life, but perverseness in it breaks the spirit.
15:5
A fool despises his father's instruction, but he who heeds admonition is prudent.
15:6
In the house of the righteous there is much

treasure, but trouble befalls the income of the wicked.

15:7

The lips of the wise spread knowledge; not so the minds of fools.

15:8

The sacrifice of the wicked is an abomination to the LORD, but the prayer of the upright is his delight.

15:9

The way of the wicked is an abomination to the LORD, but he loves him who pursues righteousness.

treasure, but trouble befalls the income of the wicked.

15:7

The lips of the wise spread knowledge; not so the minds of fools.

15:8

The sacrifice of the wicked is an abomination to the LORD, but the prayer of the upright is his delight.

15:9

The way of the wicked is an abomination to the LORD, but he loves him who pursues righteousness.

15:10
There is severe discipline for him who forsakes the way; he who hates reproof will die.
15:11
Sheol and Abaddon lie open before the LORD, how much more the hearts of men!
15:12
A scoffer does not like to be reproved; he will not go to the wise.
15:13
A glad heart makes a cheerful countenance, but by sorrow of heart the spirit is

15:10
There is severe discipline for him who forsakes the way; he who hates reproof will die.
15:11
Sheol and Abaddon lie open before the LORD how much more the hearts of men!
15:12
A scoffer does not like to be reproved; he will not go to the wise.
15:13
A glad heart makes a cheerful countenance, but by sorrow of heart the spirit is

broken.

15:14

The mind of him who has understanding seeks knowledge, but the mouths of fools feed on folly.

15:15

All the days of the afflicted are evil, but a cheerful heart has a continual feast.

15:16

Better is a little with the fear of the LORD than great treasure and trouble with it.

15:17

Better is a dinner of herbs

broken.

15:14

The mind of him who has understanding seeks knowledge, but the mouths of fools feed on folly.

15:15

All the days of the afflicted are evil, but a cheerful heart has a continual feast.

15:16

Better is a little with the fear of the LORD than great treasure and trouble with it.

15:17

Better is a dinner of herbs

where love is than a fatted ox and hatred with it.

15:18

A hot-tempered man stirs up strife, but he who is slow to anger quiets contention.

15:19

The way of a sluggard is overgrown with thorns, but the path of the upright is a level highway.

15:20

A wise son makes a glad father, but a foolish man despises his mother.

15:21

Folly is a joy to him who

where love is than a fatted ox and hatred with it.

15:18

A hot-tempered man stirs up strife, but he who is slow to anger quiets contention.

15:19

The way of a sluggard is overgrown with thorns, but the path of the upright is a level highway.

15:20

A wise son makes a glad father, but a foolish man despises his mother.

15:21

Folly is a joy to him who

has no sense, but a man of understanding walks aright.

15:22
Without counsel plans go wrong, but with many advisers they succeed.

15:23
To make an apt answer is a joy to a man, and a word in season, how good it is!

15:24
The wise man's path leads upward to life, that he may avoid Sheol beneath.

15:25
The LORD tears down the house of the proud,

has no sense, but a man of understanding walks aright.
15:22
Without counsel plans go wrong, but with many advisers they succeed.
15:23
To make an apt answer is a joy to a man, and a word in season, how good it is!
15:24
The wise man's path leads upward to life, that he may avoid Sheol beneath.
15:25
The LORD tears down the house of the proud,

but maintains the widow's boundaries.

15:26

The thoughts of the wicked are an abomination to the LORD, the words of the pure are pleasing to him.

15:27

He who is greedy for unjust gain makes trouble for his household, but he who hates bribes will live.

15:28

The mind of the righteous ponders how to answer, but the mouth of the wicked pours out evil things.

but maintains the widow's boundaries.
15:26
The thoughts of the wicked are an abomination to the LORD, the words of the pure are pleasing to him.
15:27
He who is greedy for unjust gain makes trouble for his household, but he who hates bribes will live.
15:28
The mind of the righteous ponders how to answer, but the mouth of the wicked pours out evil things.

15:29
The LORD is far from the wicked, but he hears the prayer of the righteous.

15:30
The light of the eyes rejoices the heart, and good news refreshes the bones.

15:31
He whose ear heeds wholesome admonition will abide among the wise.

15:32
He who ignores instruction despises himself, but he who heeds admonition gains

15:29
The LORD is far from the wicked, but he hears the prayer of the righteous.
15:30
The light of the eyes rejoices the heart, and good news refreshes the bones.
15:31
He whose ear heeds wholesome admonition will abide among the wise.
15:32
He who ignores instruction despises himself, but he who heeds admonition gains

understanding.

15:33

The fear of the LORD is instruction in wisdom, and humility goes before honor.

Proberbs 16

16:1

The plans of the mind belong to man, but the answer of the tongue is from the LORD.

16:2

All the ways of a man are pure in his own eyes, but the LORD weighs the spirit.

understanding.

15:33

The fear of the LORD is instruction in wisdom, and humility goes before honor.

Proberbs 16

16:1

The plans of the mind belong to man, but the answer of the tongue is from the LORD.

16:2

All the ways of a man are pure in his own eyes, but the LORD weighs the spirit.

16:3
Commit your work to the LORD, and your plans will be established.
16:4
The LORD has made everything for its purpose, even the wicked for the day of trouble.
16:5
Every one who is arrogant is an abomination to the LORD; be assured, he will not go unpunished.
16:6
By loyalty and faithfulness iniquity is atoned for, and by the fear of the

16:3
Commit your work to the LORD, and your plans will be established.
16:4
The LORD has made everything for its purpose, even the wicked for the day of trouble.
16:5
Every one who is arrogant is an abomination to the LORD; be assured, he will not go unpunished.
16:6
By loyalty and faithfulness iniquity is atoned for, and by the fear of the

LORD a man avoids evil.

16:7

When a man's ways please the LORD, he makes even his enemies to be at peace with him.

16:8

Better is a little with righteousness than great revenues with injustice.

16:9

A man's mind plans his way, but the LORD directs his steps.

16:10

Inspired decisions are on the lips of a king; his mouth does not sin in

LORD a man avoids evil.

16:7

When a man's ways please the LORD, he makes even his enemies to be at peace with him.

16:8

Better is a little with righteousness than great revenues with injustice.

16:9

A man's mind plans his way, but the LORD directs his steps.

16:10

Inspired decisions are on the lips of a king; his mouth does not sin in judgment.

16:11

A just balance and scales are the LORD's; all the weights in the bag are his work.

16:12

It is an abomination to kings to do evil, for the throne is established by righteousness.

16:13

Righteous lips are the delight of a king, and he loves him who speaks what is right.

16:14

A king's wrath is a

judgment.

16:11
A just balance and scales are the LORD's; all the weights in the bag are his work.

16:12
It is an abomination to kings to do evil, for the throne is established by righteousness.

16:13
Righteous lips are the delight of a king, and he loves him who speaks what is right.

16:14
A king's wrath is a

messenger of death, and a wise man will appease it.

16:15

In the light of a king's face there is life, and his favor is like the clouds that bring the spring rain.

16:16

To get wisdom is better than gold; to get understanding is to be chosen rather than silver.

16:17

The highway of the upright turns aside from evil; he who guards his way preserves his life.

messenger of
death, and a
wise man will
appease it.
16:15
In the light of
a king's face
there is life,
and his favor
is like the
clouds that
bring the
spring rain.

16:16
To get
wisdom is
better than
gold; to get
understanding
is to be
chosen rather
than silver.
16:17
The highway
of the upright
turns aside
from evil; he
who guards
his way
preserves his
life.

16:18
Pride goes before destruction, and a haughty spirit before a fall.

16:19
It is better to be of a lowly spirit with the poor than to divide the spoil with the proud.

16:20
He who gives heed to the word will prosper, and happy is he who trusts in the LORD.

16:21
The wise of heart is called a man of discernment, and pleasant speech increases

16:18
Pride goes before destruction, and a haughty spirit before a fall.
16:19
It is better to be of a lowly spirit with the poor than to divide the spoil with the proud.
16:20
He who gives heed to the word will prosper, and happy is he who trusts in the LORD.
16:21
The wise of heart is called a man of discernment, and pleasant speech increases

persuasiveness.
16:22
Wisdom is a fountain of life to him who has it, but folly is the chastisement of fools.
16:23
The mind of the wise makes his speech judicious, and adds persuasiveness to his lips.
16:24
Pleasant words are like a honeycomb, sweetness to the soul and health to the body.
16:25
There is a way which

persuasiveness.
16:22
Wisdom is a fountain of life to him who has it, but folly is the chastisement of fools.

16:23
The mind of the wise makes his speech judicious, and adds persuasiveness to his lips.

16:24
Pleasant words are like a honeycomb, sweetness to the soul and health to the body.

16:25
There is a way which

seems right to a man, but its end is the way to death.

16:26
A worker's appetite works for him; his mouth urges him on.

16:27
A worthless man plots evil, and his speech is like a scorching fire.

16:28
A perverse man spreads strife, and a whisperer separates close friends.

16:29
A man of violence entices his neighbor and leads him

seems right to a man, but its end is the way to death.

16:26
A worker's appetite works for him; his mouth urges him on.

16:27
A worthless man plots evil, and his speech is like a scorching fire.

16:28
A perverse man spreads strife, and a whisperer separates close friends.

16:29
A man of violence entices his neighbor and leads him

in a way that is not good.

16:30

He who winks his eyes plans perverse things, he who compresses his lips brings evil to pass.

16:31

A hoary head is a crown of glory; it is gained in a righteous life.

16:32

He who is slow to anger is better than the mighty, and he who rules his spirit than he who takes a city.

16:33

The lot is cast into the lap, but the decision is

in a way that is not good.

16:30

He who winks his eyes plans perverse things, he who compresses his lips brings evil to pass.

16:31

A hoary head is a crown of glory; it is gained in a righteous life.

16:32

He who is slow to anger is better than the mighty, and he who rules his spirit than he who takes a city.

16:33

The lot is cast into the lap, but the decision is

wholly from the LORD.

wholly from the LORD.

Proberbs 17

17:1

Better is a dry morsel with quiet than a house full of feasting with strife.

17:2

A slave who deals wisely will rule over a son who acts shamefully, and will share the inheritance as one of the brothers.

17:3

The crucible is for silver, and the furnace is for

Proberbs 17
17:1
Better is a dry morsel with quiet than a house full of feasting with strife.
17:2
A slave who deals wisely will rule over a son who acts shamefully, and will share the inheritance as one of the brothers.
17:3
The crucible is for silver, and the furnace is for

gold, and the LORD tries hearts.

17:4

An evildoer listens to wicked lips; and a liar gives heed to a mischievous tongue.

17:5

He who mocks the poor insults his Maker; he who is glad at calamity will not go unpunished.

17:6

Grandchildren are the crown of the aged, and the glory of sons is their fathers.

17:7

Fine speech is not becoming

gold, and the LORD tries hearts.

17:4

An evildoer listens to wicked lips; and a liar gives heed to a mischievous tongue.

17:5

He who mocks the poor insults his Maker; he who is glad at calamity will not go unpunished.

17:6

Grandchildren are the crown of the aged, and the glory of sons is their fathers.

17:7

Fine speech is not becoming

to a fool; still less is false speech to a prince.

17:8

A bribe is like a magic stone in the eyes of him who gives it; wherever he turns he prospers.

17:9

He who forgives an offense seeks love, but he who repeats a matter alienates a friend.

17:10

A rebuke goes deeper into a man of understanding than a hundred blows into a fool.

to a fool; still less is false speech to a prince.

17:8

A bribe is like a magic stone in the eyes of him who gives it; wherever he turns he prospers.

17:9

He who forgives an offense seeks love, but he who repeats a matter alienates a friend.

17:10

A rebuke goes deeper into a man of understanding than a hundred blows into a fool.

17:11
An evil man seeks only rebellion, and a cruel messenger will be sent against him.
17:12
Let a man meet a she-bear robbed of her cubs, rather than a fool in his folly.
17:13
If a man returns evil for good, evil will not depart from his house.
17:14
The beginning of strife is like letting out water; so quit before the quarrel breaks out.

17:11
An evil man seeks only rebellion, and a cruel messenger will be sent against him.
17:12
Let a man meet a she-bear robbed of her cubs, rather than a fool in his folly.
17:13
If a man returns evil for good, evil will not depart from his house.
17:14
The beginning of strife is like letting out water; so quit before the quarrel breaks out.

17:15
He who justifies the wicked and he who condemns the righteous are both alike an abomination to the LORD.
17:16
Why should a fool have a price in his hand to buy wisdom, when he has no mind?
17:17
A friend loves at all times, and a brother is born for adversity.
17:18
A man without sense gives a pledge, and becomes surety in the presence of

17:15
He who justifies the wicked and he who condemns the righteous are both alike an abomination to the LORD.
17:16
Why should a fool have a price in his hand to buy wisdom, when he has no mind?
17:17
A friend loves at all times, and a brother is born for adversity.
17:18
A man without sense gives a pledge, and becomes surety in the presence of

his neighbor.
17:19
He who loves transgression loves strife; he who makes his door high seeks destruction.
17:20
A man of crooked mind does not prosper, and one with a perverse tongue falls into calamity.
17:21
A stupid son is a grief to a father; and the father of a fool has no joy.
17:22
A cheerful heart is a good medicine, but a downcast

his neighbor.
17:19
He who loves transgression loves strife;
he who makes his door high seeks destruction.
17:20
A man of crooked mind does not prosper, and one with a perverse tongue falls into calamity.
17:21
A stupid son is a grief to a father;
and the father of a fool has no joy.
17:22
A cheerful heart is a good medicine, but a downcast

spirit dries up the bones.

17:23

A wicked man accepts a bribe from the bosom to pervert the ways of justice.

17:24

A man of understanding sets his face toward wisdom, but the eyes of a fool are on the ends of the earth.

17:25

A foolish son is a grief to his father and bitterness to her who bore him.

17:26

To impose a fine on a righteous man is not good;

spirit dries up the bones.

17:23

A wicked man accepts a bribe from the bosom to pervert the ways of justice.

17:24

A man of understanding sets his face toward wisdom, but the eyes of a fool are on the ends of the earth.

17:25

A foolish son is a grief to his father and bitterness to her who bore him.

17:26

To impose a fine on a righteous man is not good;

to flog noble men is wrong.

17:27

He who restrains his words has knowledge, and he who has a cool spirit is a man of understanding.

17:28

Even a fool who keeps silent is considered wise; when he closes his lips, he is deemed intelligent.

Proberbs 18

18:1

He who is estranged seeks pretexts to break out against all sound

to flog noble men is wrong.

17:27

He who restrains his words has knowledge, and he who has a cool spirit is a man of understanding.

17:28

Even a fool who keeps silent is considered wise; when he closes his lips, he is deemed intelligent.

Proberbs 18

18:1

He who is estranged seeks pretexts to break out against all sound

judgment.
18:2
A fool takes no pleasure in understanding, but only in expressing his opinion.
18:3
When wickedness comes, contempt comes also; and with dishonor comes disgrace.
18:4
The words of a man's mouth are deep waters; the fountain of wisdom is a gushing stream.
18:5
It is not good to be partial to a wicked man, or to

judgment.
18:2
A fool takes no pleasure in understanding, but only in expressing his opinion.
18:3
When wickedness comes, contempt comes also; and with dishonor comes disgrace.
18:4
The words of a man's mouth are deep waters; the fountain of wisdom is a gushing stream.
18:5
It is not good to be partial to a wicked

deprive a righteous man of justice.

18:6

A fool's lips bring strife, and his mouth invites a flogging.

18:7

A fool's mouth is his ruin, and his lips are a snare to himself.

18:8

The words of a whisperer are like delicious morsels; they go down into the inner parts of the body.

18:9

He who is slack in his work is a brother to him

man, or to deprive a righteous man of justice.

18:6

A fool's lips bring strife, and his mouth invites a flogging.

18:7

A fool's mouth is his ruin, and his lips are a snare to himself.

18:8

The words of a whisperer are like delicious morsels; they go down into the inner parts of the body.

18:9

He who is slack in his work is a brother to

who destroys.

18:10

The name of the LORD is a strong tower; the righteous man runs into it and is safe.

18:11

A rich man's wealth is his strong city, and like a high wall protecting him.

18:12

Before destruction a man's heart is haughty, but humility goes before honor.

18:13

If one gives answer before he hears, it is his folly and shame.

him who destroys.

18:10

The name of the LORD is a strong tower; the righteous man runs into it and is safe.

18:11

A rich man's wealth is his strong city, and like a high wall protecting him.

18:12

Before destruction a man's heart is haughty, but humility goes before honor.

18:13

If one gives answer before he hears, it is his folly and shame.

18:14
A man's spirit will endure sickness; but a broken spirit who can bear?

18:15
An intelligent mind acquires knowledge, and the ear of the wise seeks knowledge.

18:16
A man's gift makes room for him and brings him before great men.

18:17
He who states his case first seems right, until the other comes and examines him.

18:18
The lot puts an end to

18:14
A man's spirit will endure sickness;
but a broken spirit who can bear?

18:15
An intelligent mind acquires knowledge,
and the ear of the wise seeks knowledge.

18:16
A man's gift makes room for him and brings him before great men.

18:17
He who states his case first seems right,
until the other comes and examines him.

18:18
The lot puts an end to disputes and

disputes and decides between powerful contenders.

18:19

A brother helped is like a strong city, but quarreling is like the bars of a castle.

18:20

From the fruit of his mouth a man is satisfied; he is satisfied by the yield of his lips.

18:21

Death and life are in the power of the tongue, and those who love it will eat its fruits.

18:22

He who finds

decides between powerful contenders.

18:19

A brother helped is like a strong city, but quarreling is like the bars of a castle.

18:20

From the fruit of his mouth a man is satisfied; he is satisfied by the yield of his lips.

18:21

Death and life are in the power of the tongue, and those who love it will eat its fruits.

18:22

He who finds
a wife finds a

a wife finds a good thing, and obtains favor from the LORD.

good thing, and obtains favor from the LORD.

18:23

The poor use entreaties, but the rich answer roughly.

The poor use entreaties, but the rich answer roughly.

18:24

There are friends who pretend to be friends, but there is a friend who sticks closer than a brother.

There are friends who pretend to be friends, but there is a friend who sticks closer than a brother.

Proberbs **19**

Proberbs **19**

19:1

Better is a poor man who walks in his integrity than a man who is

Better is a poor man who walks in his integrity than a man who is perverse in speech, and is a fool.

19:2

It is not good for a man to be without knowledge, and he who makes haste with his feet misses his way.

19:3

When a man's folly brings his way to ruin, his heart rages against the LORD.

19:4

Wealth brings many new friends, but a poor man is deserted by his friend.

19:5

A false witness will not go

perverse in speech, and is a fool.

19:2

It is not good for a man to be without knowledge, and he who makes haste with his feet misses his way.

19:3

When a man's folly brings his way to ruin, his heart rages against the LORD.

19:4

Wealth brings many new friends, but a poor man is deserted by his friend.

19:5

A false witness will not go

unpunished, and he who utters lies will not escape.

19:6

Many seek the favor of a generous man, and every one is a friend to a man who gives gifts.

19:7

All a poor man's brothers hate him; how much more do his friends go far from him! He pursues them with words, but does not have them.

19:8

He who gets wisdom loves himself; he who keeps

unpunished, and he who utters lies will not escape.

19:6

Many seek the favor of a generous man, and every one is a friend to a man who gives gifts.

19:7

All a poor man's brothers hate him; how much more do his friends go far from him! He pursues them with words, but does not have them.

19:8

He who gets wisdom loves himself; he who keeps

understanding will prosper.

19:9

A false witness will not go unpunished, and he who utters lies will perish.

19:10

It is not fitting for a fool to live in luxury, much less for a slave to rule over princes.

19:11

Good sense makes a man slow to anger, and it is his glory to overlook an offense.

19:12

A king's wrath is like the growling of a lion, but his favor

understanding will prosper.

19:9

A false witness will not go unpunished, and he who utters lies will perish.

19:10

It is not fitting for a fool to live in luxury, much less for a slave to rule over princes.

19:11

Good sense makes a man slow to anger, and it is his glory to overlook an offense.

19:12

A king's wrath is like the growling of a lion, but his favor is *is like dew upon the grass.*

19:13

A foolish son is ruin to his father, and a wife's quarreling is a continual dripping of rain.

19:14

House and wealth are inherited from fathers, but a prudent wife is from the LORD.

19:15

Slothfulness casts into a deep sleep, and an idle person will suffer hunger.

19:16

He who keeps the commandment keeps his life;

like dew upon the grass.

19:13

A foolish son is ruin to his father, and a wife's quarreling is a continual dripping of rain.

19:14

House and wealth are inherited from fathers, but a prudent wife is from the LORD.

19:15

Slothfulness casts into a deep sleep, and an idle person will suffer hunger.

19:16

He who keeps the commandment keeps his life;

he who despises the word will die.

19:17

He who is kind to the poor lends to the LORD, and he will repay him for his deed.

19:18

Discipline your son while there is hope; do not set your heart on his destruction.

19:19

A man of great wrath will pay the penalty; for if you deliver him, you will only have to do it again.

he who despises the word will die.

19:17

He who is kind to the poor lends to the LORD, and he will repay him for his deed.

19:18

Discipline your son while there is hope; do not set your heart on his destruction.

19:19

A man of great wrath will pay the penalty; for if you deliver him, you will only have to do it again.

19:20
Listen to advice and accept instruction, that you may gain wisdom for the future.
19:21
Many are the plans in the mind of a man, but it is the purpose of the LORD that will be established.
19:22
What is desired in a man is loyalty, and a poor man is better than a liar.
19:23
The fear of the LORD leads to life; and he who has it rests satisfied; he

19:20
Listen to advice and accept instruction, that you may gain wisdom for the future.
19:21
Many are the plans in the mind of a man, but it is the purpose of the LORD that will be established.
19:22
What is desired in a man is loyalty, and a poor man is better than a liar.
19:23
The fear of the LORD leads to life; and he who has it rests satisfied; he will not be

will not be visited by harm.

19:24

The sluggard buries his hand in the dish, and will not even bring it back to his mouth.

19:25

Strike a scoffer, and the simple will learn prudence; reprove a man of understanding, and he will gain knowledge.

19:26

He who does violence to his father and chases away his mother is a son who causes

visited by harm.

19:24

The sluggard buries his hand in the dish, and will not even bring it back to his mouth.

19:25

Strike a scoffer, and the simple will learn prudence; reprove a man of understanding, and he will gain knowledge.

19:26

He who does violence to his father and chases away his mother is a son who causes

shame and brings reproach.
19:27
Cease, my son, to hear instruction only to stray from the words of knowledge.
19:28
A worthless witness mocks at justice, and the mouth of the wicked devours iniquity.
19:29
Condemnation is ready for scoffers, and flogging for the backs of fools.

shame and brings reproach.
19:27
Cease, my son, to hear instruction only to stray from the words of knowledge.
19:28
A worthless witness mocks at justice, and the mouth of the wicked devours iniquity.
19:29
Condemnation is ready for scoffers, and flogging for the backs of fools.

Proberbs 20

20:1
Wine is a mocker, strong drink a brawler; and whoever is led astray by it is not wise.

20:2
The dread wrath of a king is like the growling of a lion; he who provokes him to anger forfeits his life.

20:3
It is an honor for a man to keep aloof from strife; but every fool will be quarreling.

20:4
The sluggard does not plow

Proberbs 20

20:1
Wine is a mocker, strong drink a brawler; and whoever is led astray by it is not wise.

20:2
The dread wrath of a king is like the growling of a lion; he who provokes him to anger forfeits his life.

20:3
It is an honor for a man to keep aloof from strife; but every fool will be quarreling.

20:4
The sluggard does not plow

in the autumn; he will seek at harvest and have nothing.

20:5

The purpose in a man's mind is like deep water, but a man of understanding will draw it out.

20:6

Many a man proclaims his own loyalty, but a faithful man who can find?

20:7

A righteous man who walks in his integrity— blessed are his sons after him!

in the autumn; he will seek at harvest and have nothing.

20:5

The purpose in a man's mind is like deep water, but a man of understanding will draw it out.

20:6

Many a man proclaims his own loyalty, but a faithful man who can find?

20:7

A righteous man who walks in his integrity— blessed are his sons after him!

20:8
A king who sits on the throne of judgment winnows all evil with his eyes.

20:9
Who can say, "I have made my heart clean; I am pure from my sin"?

20:10
Diverse weights and diverse measures are both alike an abomination to the LORD.

20:11
Even a child makes himself known by his acts, whether what he does is pure and right.

20:8
A king who sits on the throne of judgment winnows all evil with his eyes.
20:9
Who can say, "I have made my heart clean; I am pure from my sin"?
20:10
Diverse weights and diverse measures are both alike an abomination to the LORD.
20:11
Even a child makes himself known by his acts, whether what he does is pure and right.

20:12
The hearing ear and the seeing eye, the LORD has made them both.

20:13
Love not sleep, lest you come to poverty; open your eyes, and you will have plenty of bread.

20:14
"It is bad, it is bad," says the buyer; but when he goes away, then he boasts.

20:15
There is gold, and abundance of costly stones; but the lips of knowledge are a precious jewel.

20:12
The hearing ear and the seeing eye, the LORD has made them both.

20:13
Love not sleep, lest you come to poverty; open your eyes, and you will have plenty of bread.

20:14
"It is bad, it is bad," says the buyer; but when he goes away, then he boasts.

20:15
There is gold, and abundance of costly stones; but the lips of knowledge are a precious jewel.

20:16
Take a man's garment when he has given surety for a stranger, and hold him in pledge when he gives surety for foreigners.
20:17
Bread gained by deceit is sweet to a man, but afterward his mouth will be full of gravel.
20:18
Plans are established by counsel; by wise guidance wage war.
20:19
He who goes about gossiping reveals secrets;

20:16
Take a man's garment when he has given surety for a stranger, and hold him in pledge when he gives surety for foreigners.
20:17
Bread gained by deceit is sweet to a man, but afterward his mouth will be full of gravel.
20:18
Plans are established by counsel; by wise guidance wage war.
20:19
He who goes about gossiping reveals secrets;

therefore do not associate with one who speaks foolishly.

therefore do not associate with one who speaks foolishly.

20:20

If one curses his father or his mother, his lamp will be put out in utter darkness.

If one curses his father or his mother, his lamp will be put out in utter darkness.

20:21

An inheritance gotten hastily in the beginning will in the end not be blessed.

An inheritance gotten hastily in the beginning will in the end not be blessed.

20:22

Do not say, "I will repay evil"; wait for the LORD, and he will help you.

Do not say, "I will repay evil"; wait for the LORD, and he will help you.

20:23
Diverse weights are an abomination to the LORD, and false scales are not good.

20:24
A man's steps are ordered by the LORD; how then can man understand his way?

20:25
It is a snare for a man to say rashly, "It is holy," and to reflect only after making his vows.

20:26
A wise king winnows the wicked, and drives the

20:23
Diverse weights are an abomination to the LORD, and false scales are not good.

20:24
A man's steps are ordered by the LORD; how then can man understand his way?

20:25
It is a snare for a man to say rashly, "It is holy," and to reflect only after making his vows.

20:26
A wise king winnows the wicked, and drives the

wheel over them.

20:27

The spirit of man is the lamp of the LORD, searching all his innermost parts.

20:28

Loyalty and faithfulness preserve the king, and his throne is upheld by righteousness.

20:29

The glory of young men is their strength, but the beauty of old men is their gray hair.

20:30

Blows that wound cleanse

wheel over them.

20:27

The spirit of man is the lamp of the LORD, searching all his innermost parts.

20:28

Loyalty and faithfulness preserve the king, and his throne is upheld by righteousness.

20:29

The glory of young men is their strength, but the beauty of old men is their gray hair.

20:30

Blows that wound cleanse

away evil; strokes make clean the innermost parts.

Proberbs 21

21:1

The king's heart is a stream of water in the hand of the LORD; he turns it wherever he will.

21:2

Every way of a man is right in his own eyes, but the LORD weighs the heart.

21:3

To do righteousness and justice is more acceptable to

away evil; strokes make clean the innermost parts.

Proberbs 21

21:1

The king's heart is a stream of water in the hand of the LORD; he turns it wherever he will.

21:2

Every way of a man is right in his own eyes, but the LORD weighs the heart.

21:3

To do righteousness and justice is more acceptable to

the LORD than sacrifice.

21:4

Haughty eyes and a proud heart, the lamp of the wicked, are sin.

21:5

The plans of the diligent lead surely to abundance, but every one who is hasty comes only to want.

21:6

The getting of treasures by a lying tongue is a fleeting vapor and a snare of death.

21:7

The violence of the wicked will sweep them away,

the LORD
than sacrifice.
21:4
Haughty eyes
and a proud
heart, the
lamp of the
wicked, are
sin.

21:5
The plans of
the diligent
lead surely to
abundance,
but every one
who is hasty
comes only to
want.
21:6
The getting of
treasures by a
lying tongue
is a fleeting
vapor and a
snare of
death.

21:7
The violence
of the wicked
will sweep
them away,

because they refuse to do what is just.

21:8

The way of the guilty is crooked, but the conduct of the pure is right.

21:9

It is better to live in a corner of the housetop than in a house shared with a contentious woman.

21:10

The soul of the wicked desires evil; his neighbor finds no mercy in his eyes.

21:11

When a scoffer is punished, the simple

because they refuse to do what is just.

21:8

The way of the guilty is crooked, but the conduct of the pure is right.

21:9

It is better to live in a corner of the housetop than in a house shared with a contentious woman.

21:10

The soul of the wicked desires evil; his neighbor finds no mercy in his eyes.

21:11

When a scoffer is punished, the simple

becomes wise; when a wise man is instructed, he gains knowledge.

21:12

The righteous observes the house of the wicked; the wicked are cast down to ruin.

21:13

He who closes his ear to the cry of the poor will himself cry out and not be heard.

21:14

A gift in secret averts anger; and a bribe in the bosom, strong wrath.

becomes wise; when a wise man is instructed, he gains knowledge.

21:12

The righteous observes the house of the wicked; the wicked are cast down to ruin.

21:13

He who closes his ear to the cry of the poor will himself cry out and not be heard.

21:14

A gift in secret averts anger; and a bribe in the bosom, strong wrath.

21:15

When justice is done, it is a joy to the righteous, but dismay to evildoers.

21:16

A man who wanders from the way of understanding will rest in the assembly of the dead.

21:17

He who loves pleasure will be a poor man; he who loves wine and oil will not be rich.

21:18

He wicked is a ransom for the righteous, and the faithless for the upright.

21:15
When justice is done, it is a joy to the righteous, but dismay to evildoers.
21:16
A man who wanders from the way of understanding will rest in the assembly of the dead.
21:17
He who loves pleasure will be a poor man; he who loves wine and oil will not be rich.
21:18
He wicked is a ransom for the righteous, and the faithless for the upright.

21:19

It is better to live in a desert land than with a contentious and fretful woman.

21:20

Precious treasure remains in a wise man's dwelling, but a foolish man devours it.

21:21

He who pursues righteousness and kindness will find life and honor.

21:22

A wise man scales the city of the mighty and brings down the stronghold in which they trust.

21:19
It is better to live in a desert land than with a contentious and fretful woman.
21:20
Precious treasure remains in a wise man's dwelling, but a foolish man devours it.
21:21
He who pursues righteousness and kindness will find life and honor.
21:22
A wise man scales the city of the mighty and brings down the stronghold in which they trust.

21:23
He who keeps his mouth and his tongue keeps himself out of trouble.
21:24
"Scoffer" is the name of the proud, haughty man who acts with arrogant pride.
21:25
The desire of the sluggard kills him for his hands refuse to labor.
21:26
All day long the wicked covets, but the righteous gives and does not hold back.

21:23
He who keeps his mouth and his tongue keeps himself out of trouble.
21:24
"Scoffer" is the name of the proud, haughty man who acts with arrogant pride.
21:25
The desire of the sluggard kills him for his hands refuse to labor.
21:26
All day long the wicked covets, but the righteous gives and does not hold back.

21:27
The sacrifice of the wicked is an abomination; how much more when he brings it with evil intent.

21:28
A false witness will perish, but the word of a man who hears will endure.

21:29
A wicked man puts on a bold face, but an upright man considers his ways.

21:30
No wisdom, no understanding, no counsel, can avail against the LORD.

21:27
The sacrifice of the wicked is an abomination; how much more when he brings it with evil intent.
21:28
A false witness will perish, but the word of a man who hears will endure.
21:29
A wicked man puts on a bold face, but an upright man considers his ways.
21:30
No wisdom, no understanding, no counsel, can avail against the LORD.

21:31
The horse is made ready for the day of battle, but the victory belongs to the LORD.

Proberbs 22

22:1
A good name is to be chosen rather than great riches, and favor is better than silver or gold.

22:2
The rich and the poor meet together; the LORD is the maker of them all.

21:31
The horse is made ready for the day of battle, but the victory belongs to the LORD.

Proberbs 22

22:1
A good name is to be chosen rather than great riches, and favor is better than silver or gold.

22:2
The rich and the poor meet together; the LORD is the maker of them all.

22:3
A prudent man sees danger and hides himself; but the simple go on, and suffer for it.

22:4
The reward for humility and fear of the LORD is riches and honor and life.

22:5
Thorns and snares are in the way of the perverse; he who guards himself will keep far from them.

22:6
Train up a child in the way he should go, and when he is old he

22:3
A prudent man sees danger and hides himself; but the simple go on, and suffer for it.

22:4
The reward for humility and fear of the LORD is riches and honor and life.

22:5
Thorns and snares are in the way of the perverse; he who guards himself will keep far from them.

22:6
Train up a child in the way he should go, and when he is old he

will not depart from it.

22:7

The rich rules over the poor, and the borrower is the slave of the lender.

22:8

He who sows injustice will reap calamity, and the rod of his fury will fail.

22:9

He who has a bountiful eye will be blessed, for he shares his bread with the poor.

22:10

Drive out a scoffer, and strife will go out, and quarreling and abuse will

will not depart from it.

22:7

The rich rules over the poor, and the borrower is the slave of the lender.

22:8

He who sows injustice will reap calamity, and the rod of his fury will fail.

22:9

He who has a bountiful eye will be blessed, for he shares his bread with the poor.

22:10

Drive out a scoffer, and strife will go out, and quarreling and abuse will *cease.*

22:11

He who loves purity of heart, and whose speech is gracious, will have the king as his friend.

22:12

The eyes of the LORD keep watch over knowledge, but he overthrows the words of the faithless.

22:13

The sluggard says, "There is a lion outside! I shall be slain in the streets!"

22:14

The mouth of a loose woman is a

cease.

22:11

He who loves purity of heart, and whose speech is gracious, will have the king as his friend.

22:12

The eyes of the LORD keep watch over knowledge, but he overthrows the words of the faithless.

22:13

The sluggard says, "There is a lion outside! I shall be slain in the streets!"

22:14

The mouth of a loose woman is a

deep pit; he with whom the LORD is angry will fall into it.

22:15
Folly is bound up in the heart of a child, but the rod of discipline drives it far from him.

22:16
He who oppresses the poor to increase his own wealth, or gives to the rich, will only come to want.

22:17
Incline your ear, and hear the words of the wise, and apply your mind to my

deep pit; he with whom the LORD is angry will fall into it.

22:15
Folly is bound up in the heart of a child, but the rod of discipline drives it far from him.

22:16
He who oppresses the poor to increase his own wealth, or gives to the rich, will only come to want.

22:17
Incline your ear, and hear the words of the wise, and apply your mind to my

knowledge;
22:18
for it will be pleasant if you keep them within you, if all of them are ready on your lips.
22:19
That your trust may be in the LORD, I have made them known to you today, even to you.
22:20
Have I not written for you thirty sayings of admonition and knowledge,
22:21
to show you what is right and true, that you may

knowledge;
22:18
for it will be pleasant if you keep them within you, if all of them are ready on your lips.
22:19
That your trust may be in the LORD, I have made them known to you today, even to you.
22:20
Have I not written for you thirty sayings of admonition and knowledge,
22:21
to show you what is right and true, that you may

give a true answer to those who sent you?

22:22

Do not rob the poor, because he is poor, or crush the afflicted at the gate;

22:23

for the LORD will plead their cause and despoil of life those who despoil them.

22:24

Make no friendship with a man given to anger, nor go with a wrathful man,

22:25

lest you learn his ways and entangle yourself in a

give a true answer to those who sent you?

22:22

Do not rob the poor, because he is poor, or crush the afflicted at the gate;

22:23

for the LORD will plead their cause and despoil of life those who despoil them.

22:24

Make no friendship with a man given to anger, nor go with a wrathful man,

22:25

lest you learn his ways and entangle yourself in a

snare.
22:26
Be not one of those who give pledges, who become surety for debts.
22:27
If you have nothing with which to pay, why should your bed be taken from under you?
22:28
Remove not the ancient landmark which your fathers have set.
22:29
Do you see a man skilful in his work? he will stand before kings; he will not

snare.
22:26
Be not one of those who give pledges, who become surety for debts.
22:27
If you have nothing with which to pay, why should your bed be taken from under you?
22:28
Remove not the ancient landmark which your fathers have set.
22:29
Do you see a man skilful in his work? he will stand before kings; he will not

stand before obscure men.

stand before
obscure men.

Proberbs 23

23:1

When you sit down to eat with a ruler, observe carefully what is before you;

23:2

and put a knife to your throat if you are a man given to appetite.

23:3

Do not desire his delicacies, for they are deceptive food.

23:4

Do not toil to acquire

Proberbs 23
23:1
When you sit
down to eat
with a ruler,
observe
carefully what
is before you;
23:2
and put a
knife to your
throat if you
are a man
given to
appetite.
23:3
Do not desire
his delicacies,
for they are
deceptive
food.
23:4
Do not toil to
acquire

wealth; be wise enough to desist.

23:5

When your eyes light upon it, it is gone; for suddenly it takes to itself wings, flying like an eagle toward heaven.

23:6

Do not eat the bread of a man who is stingy; do not desire his delicacies;

23:7

for he is like one who is inwardly reckoning. "Eat and drink!" he says to you; but his heart is not

wealth; be wise enough to desist.

23:5

When your eyes light upon it, it is gone; for suddenly it takes to itself wings, flying like an eagle toward heaven.

23:6

Do not eat the bread of a man who is stingy; do not desire his delicacies;

23:7

for he is like one who is inwardly reckoning. "Eat and drink!" he says to you; but his heart is not

with you.
23:8
You will vomit up the morsels which you have eaten, and waste your pleasant words.
23:9
Do not speak in the hearing of a fool, for he will despise the wisdom of your words.
23:10
Do not remove an ancient landmark or enter the fields of the fatherless;
23:11
for their Redeemer is strong; he will plead their cause

with you.
23:8
You will vomit up the morsels which you have eaten, and waste your pleasant words.
23:9
Do not speak in the hearing of a fool, for he will despise the wisdom of your words.
23:10
Do not remove an ancient landmark or enter the fields of the fatherless;
23:11
for their Redeemer is strong; he will plead their

against you.

23:12

Apply your mind to instruction and your ear to words of knowledge.

23:13

Do not withhold discipline from a child; if you beat him with a rod, he will not die.

23:14

If you beat him with the rod you will save his life from Sheol.

23:15

My son, if your heart is wise, my heart too will be glad.

cause
against you.
23:12
Apply your mind to instruction and your ear to words of knowledge.
23:13
Do not withhold discipline from a child; if you beat him with a rod, he will not die.
23:14
If you beat him with the rod you will save his life from Sheol.
23:15
My son, if your heart is wise, my heart too will be glad.

23:16
My soul will rejoice when your lips speak what is right.

23:17
Let not your heart envy sinners, but continue in the fear of the LORD all the day.

23:18
Surely there is a future, and your hope will not be cut off.

23:19
Hear, my son, and be wise, and direct your mind in the way.

23:16
My soul will rejoice when your lips speak what is right.

23:17
Let not your heart envy sinners, but continue in the fear of the LORD all the day.

23:18
Surely there is a future, and your hope will not be cut off.

23:19
Hear, my son, and be wise, and direct your mind in the way.

23:20
Be not among winebibbers, or among gluttonous eaters of meat;

23:21
for the drunkard and the glutton will come to poverty, and drowsiness will clothe a man with rags.

23:22
Hearken to your father who begot you, and do not despise your mother when she is old.

23:23
Buy truth, and do not sell it; buy wisdom, instruction, and understanding.

23:20
Be not among winebibbers, or among gluttonous eaters of meat;

23:21
for the drunkard and the glutton will come to poverty, and drowsiness will clothe a man with rags.

23:22
Hearken to your father who begot you, and do not despise your mother when she is old.

23:23
Buy truth, and do not sell it; buy wisdom, instruction, and understanding.

23:24
The father of the righteous will greatly rejoice; he who begets a wise son will be glad in him.

23:25
Let your father and mother be glad, let her who bore you rejoice.

23:26
My son, give me your heart, and let your eyes observe my ways.

23:27
For a harlot is a deep pit; an adventuress is a narrow well.

23:24
The father of the righteous will greatly rejoice; he who begets a wise son will be glad in him.

23:25
Let your father and mother be glad, let her who bore you rejoice.

23:26
My son, give me your heart, and let your eyes observe my ways.

23:27
For a harlot is a deep pit; an adventuress is a narrow well.

23:28
She lies in wait like a robber and increases the faithless among men.

23:29
Who has woe? Who has sorrow? Who has strife? Who has complaining? Who has wounds without cause? Who has redness of eyes?

23:30
Those who tarry long over wine, those who go to try mixed wine.

23:31
Do not look at wine when it is red, when it

23:28
She lies in wait like a robber and increases the faithless among men.
23:29
Who has woe? Who has sorrow? Who has strife? Who has complaining? Who has wounds without cause? Who has redness of eyes?
23:30
Those who tarry long over wine, those who go to try mixed wine.
23:31
Do not look at wine when it is red, when it

sparkles in the cup and goes down smoothly.

23:32
At the last it bites like a serpent, and stings like an adder.

23:33
Your eyes will see strange things, and your mind utter perverse things.

23:34
You will be like one who lies down in the midst of the sea, like one who lies on the top of a mast.

23:35
"They struck me," you will say, "but I was not hurt;

sparkles in the cup and goes down smoothly.
23:32
At the last it bites like a serpent, and stings like an adder.
23:33
Your eyes will see strange things, and your mind utter perverse things.
23:34
You will be like one who lies down in the midst of the sea, like one who lies on the top of a mast.
23:35
"They struck me," you will say, "but I was not hurt;

they beat me, but I did not feel it. When shall I awake? I will seek another drink."

Proverbs 24

24:1
Be not envious of evil men, nor desire to be with them;

24:2
for their minds devise violence, and their lips talk of mischief.

24:3
By wisdom a house is built, and by understanding it is established;

they beat me, but I did not feel it. When shall I awake? I will seek another drink."

Proberbs 24

24:1
Be not envious of evil men, nor desire to be with them;

24:2
for their minds devise violence, and their lips talk of mischief.

24:3
By wisdom a house is built, and by understanding it is established;

24:4
by knowledge the rooms are filled with all precious and pleasant riches.

24:5
A wise man is mightier than a strong man, and a man of knowledge than he who has strength;

24:6
for by wise guidance you can wage your war, and in abundance of counselors there is victory.

24:7
Wisdom is too high for a fool; in the gate he does not open his mouth.

24:4
by knowledge the rooms are filled with all precious and pleasant riches.

24:5
A wise man is mightier than a strong man, and a man of knowledge than he who has strength;

24:6
for by wise guidance you can wage your war, and in abundance of counselors there is victory.

24:7
Wisdom is too high for a fool; in the gate he does not open his mouth.

24:8
He who plans to do evil will be called a mischief-maker.

24:9
The devising of folly is sin, and the scoffer is an abomination to men.

24:10
If you faint in the day of adversity, your strength is small.

24:11
Rescue those who are being taken away to death; hold back those who are stumbling to the slaughter.

24:8
He who plans to do evil will be called a mischief-maker.

24:9
The devising of folly is sin, and the scoffer is an abomination to men.

24:10
If you faint in the day of adversity, your strength is small.

24:11
Rescue those who are being taken away to death; hold back those who are stumbling to the slaughter.

24:12

If you say, "Behold, we did not know this," does not he who weighs the heart perceive it? Does not he who keeps watch over your soul know it, and will he not requite man according to his work?

24:13

My son, eat honey, for it is good, and the drippings of the honeycomb are sweet to your taste.

24:14

Know that wisdom is such to your soul; if you find it,

24:12

If you say, "Behold, we did not know this," does not he who weighs the heart perceive it? Does not he who keeps watch over your soul know it, and will he not requite man according to his work?

24:13

My son, eat honey, for it is good, and the drippings of the honeycomb are sweet to your taste.

24:14

Know that wisdom is such to your soul; if you find it,

there will be a future, and your hope will not be cut off.

24:15

Lie not in wait as a wicked man against the dwelling of the righteous; do not violence to his home;

24:16

for a righteous man falls seven times, and rises again; but the wicked are overthrown by calamity.

24:17

Do not rejoice when your enemy falls, and let not your heart be glad when

there will be a future, and your hope will not be cut off.

24:15

Lie not in wait as a wicked man against the dwelling of the righteous; do not violence to his home;

24:16

for a righteous man falls seven times, and rises again; but the wicked are overthrown by calamity.

24:17

Do not rejoice when your enemy falls, and let not your heart be glad when

he stumbles;
24:18
lest the LORD see it, and
be displeased, and turn
away his anger from him.
24:19
Fret not yourself because of
evildoers, and be not
envious of the wicked;
24:20
for the evil man has no
future; the lamp of the
wicked will be put out.
24:21
My son, fear the LORD
and the king, and do not
disobey either of them;

he stumbles;
24:18
lest the LORD
see it, and be
displeased,
and turn away
his anger
from him.
24:19
Fret not
yourself
because of
evildoers, and
be not
envious of the
wicked;
24:20
for the evil
man has no
future; the
lamp of the
wicked will be
put out.
24:21
My son, fear
the LORD and
the king, and
do not
disobey either
of them;

24:22
for disaster from them will rise suddenly, and who knows the ruin that will come from them both?

24:23
These also are sayings of the wise. Partiality in judging is not good.

24:24
He who says to the wicked, "You are innocent," will be cursed by peoples, abhorred by nations;

24:25
but those who rebuke the wicked will have delight, and a good blessing will be

24:22
for disaster from them will rise suddenly, and who knows the ruin that will come from them both?

24:23
These also are sayings of the wise. Partiality in judging is not good.

24:24
He who says to the wicked, "You are innocent," will be cursed by peoples, abhorred by nations;

24:25
but those who rebuke the wicked will have delight, and a good blessing will be

upon them.

24:26

He who gives a right answer kisses the lips.

24:27

Prepare your work outside, get everything ready for you in the field; and after that build your house.

24:28

Be not a witness against your neighbor without cause, and do not deceive with your lips.

24:29

Do not say, "I will do to him as he has done to me; I will pay the man back

upon them.

24:26

He who gives a right answer kisses the lips.

24:27

Prepare your work outside, get everything ready for you in the field; and after that build your house.

24:28

Be not a witness against your neighbor without cause, and do not deceive with your lips.

24:29

Do not say, "I will do to him as he has done to me; I will pay the man back for

for what he has done."

24:30

I passed by the field of a sluggard, by the vineyard of a man without sense;

24:31

and lo, it was all overgrown with thorns; the ground was covered with nettles, and its stone wall was broken down.

24:32

Then I saw and considered it; I looked and received instruction.

24:33

A little sleep, a little slumber, a little folding

what he has done."

24:30

I passed by the field of a sluggard, by the vineyard of a man without sense;

24:31

and lo, it was all overgrown with thorns; the ground was covered with nettles, and its stone wall was broken down.

24:32

Then I saw and considered it; I looked and received instruction.

24:33

A little sleep, a little slumber, a little folding

of the hands to rest,
24:34
and poverty will come upon you like a robber, and want like an armed man.

Proberbs 25
25:1
These also are proverbs of Solomon which the men of Hezekiah king of Judah copied.
25:2
It is the glory of God to conceal things, but the glory of kings is to search things out.

of the hands to rest,
24:34
and poverty will come upon you like a robber, and want like an armed man.

Proberbs 25
25:1
These also are proverbs of Solomon which the men of Hezekiah king of Judah copied.
25:2
It is the glory of God to conceal things, but the glory of kings is to search things out.

25:3
As the heavens for height, and the earth for depth, so the mind of kings is unsearchable.
25:4
Take away the dross from the silver, and the smith has material for a vessel;
25:5
take away the wicked from the presence of the king, and his throne will be established in righteousness.
25:6
Do not put yourself forward in the king's presence or stand in the

25:3
As the heavens for height, and the earth for depth, so the mind of kings is unsearchable.
25:4
Take away the dross from the silver, and the smith has material for a vessel;
25:5
take away the wicked from the presence of the king, and his throne will be established in righteousness.
25:6
Do not put yourself forward in the king's presence or stand in the

place of the great;

25:7

for it is better to be told, "Come up here," than to be put lower in the presence of the prince. What your eyes have seen

25:8

do not hastily bring into court; for what will you do in the end, when your neighbor puts you to shame?

25:9

Argue your case with your neighbor himself, and do not disclose another's

place of the great;

25:7

for it is better to be told, "Come up here," than to be put lower in the presence of the prince. What your eyes have seen

25:8

do not hastily bring into court; for what will you do in the end, when your neighbor puts you to shame?

25:9

Argue your case with your neighbor himself, and do not disclose another's *secret;*

25:10

lest he who hears you bring shame upon you, and your ill repute have no end.

25:11

A word fitly spoken is like apples of gold in a setting of silver.

25:12

Like a gold ring or an ornament of gold is a wise reprover to a listening ear.

25:13

Like the cold of snow in the time of harvest is a faithful messenger to those

secret;
25:10
lest he who hears you bring shame upon you, and your ill repute have no end.
25:11
A word fitly spoken is like apples of gold in a setting of silver.
25:12
Like a gold ring or an ornament of gold is a wise reprover to a listening ear.
25:13
Like the cold of snow in the time of harvest is a faithful messenger to those

who send him, he refreshes the spirit of his masters.

25:14

Like clouds and wind without rain is a man who boasts of a gift he does not give.

25:15

With patience a ruler may be persuaded, and a soft tongue will break a bone.

25:16

If you have found honey, eat only enough for you, lest you be sated with it and vomit it.

25:17

Let your foot be seldom in

who send him, he refreshes the spirit of his masters.

25:14

Like clouds and wind without rain is a man who boasts of a gift he does not give.

25:15

With patience a ruler may be persuaded, and a soft tongue will break a bone.

25:16

If you have found honey, eat only enough for you, lest you be sated with it and vomit it.

25:17

Let your foot be seldom in

your neighbor's house, lest he become weary of you and hate you.

25:18

A man who bears false witness against his neighbor is like a war club, or a sword, or a sharp arrow.

25:19

Trust in a faithless man in time of trouble is like a bad tooth or a foot that slips.

25:20

He who sings songs to a heavy heart is like one who takes off a garment on a

your neighbor's house, lest he become weary of you and hate you.

25:18

A man who bears false witness against his neighbor is like a war club, or a sword, or a sharp arrow.

25:19

Trust in a faithless man in time of trouble is like a bad tooth or a foot that slips.

25:20

He who sings songs to a heavy heart is like one who takes off a garment on a

cold day, and like vinegar
on a wound.
25:21
If your enemy is hungry,
give him bread to eat; and
if he is thirsty, give him
water to drink;
25:22
for you will heap coals of
fire on his head, and the
LORD will reward you.
25:23
The north wind brings
forth rain; and a backbiting
tongue, angry looks.
25:24
It is better to live in a
corner of the housetop than

cold day, and
like vinegar
on a wound.
25:21
If your enemy
is hungry,
give him
bread to eat;
and if he is
thirsty, give
him water to
drink;
25:22
for you will
heap coals of
fire on his
head, and the
LORD will
reward you.
25:23
The north
wind brings
forth rain;
and a
backbiting
tongue, angry
looks.
25:24
It is better to
live in a
corner of the
housetop than

in a house shared with a contentious woman.

25:25

Like cold water to a thirsty soul, so is good news from a far country.

25:26

Like a muddied spring or a polluted fountain is a righteous man who gives way before the wicked.

25:27

It is not good to eat much honey, so be sparing of complimentary words.

25:28

A man without self-control is

in a house shared with a contentious woman.

25:25

Like cold water to a thirsty soul, so is good news from a far country.

25:26

Like a muddied spring or a polluted fountain is a righteous man who gives way before the wicked.

25:27

It is not good to eat much honey, so be sparing of complimentary words.

25:28

A man without self-control is

like a city broken into and left without walls.

like a city broken into and left without walls.

Proberbs **26**

26:1

Like snow in summer or rain in harvest, so honor is not fitting for a fool.

26:2

Like a sparrow in its flitting, like a swallow in its flying, a curse that is causeless does not alight.

26:3

A whip for the horse, a bridle for the ass, and a rod for the back of fools.

Proberbs **26**

26:1

Like snow in summer or rain in harvest, so honor is not fitting for a fool.

26:2

Like a sparrow in its flitting, like a swallow in its flying, a curse that is causeless does not alight.

26:3

A whip for the horse, a bridle for the ass, and a rod for the back of fools.

26:4

Answer not a fool according to his folly, lest you be like him yourself.

26:5

Answer a fool according to his folly, lest he be wise in his own eyes.

26:6

He who sends a message by the hand of a fool cuts off his own feet and drinks violence.

26:7

Like a lame man's legs, which hang useless, is a proverb in the mouth of fools.

26:4

Answer not a fool according to his folly, lest you be like him yourself.

26:5

Answer a fool according to his folly, lest he be wise in his own eyes.

26:6

He who sends a message by the hand of a fool cuts off his own feet and drinks violence.

26:7

Like a lame man's legs, which hang useless, is a proverb in the mouth of fools.

26:8
Like one who binds the stone in the sling is he who gives honor to a fool.

26:9
Like a thorn that goes up into the hand of a drunkard is a proverb in the mouth of fools.

26:10
Like an archer who wounds everybody is he who hires a passing fool or drunkard.

26:11
Like a dog that returns to his vomit is a fool that repeats his folly.

26:8
Like one who binds the stone in the sling is he who gives honor to a fool.

26:9
Like a thorn that goes up into the hand of a drunkard is a proverb in the mouth of fools.

26:10
Like an archer who wounds everybody is he who hires a passing fool or drunkard.

26:11
Like a dog that returns to his vomit is a fool that repeats his folly.

26:12
Do you see a man who is wise in his own eyes? There is more hope for a fool than for him.

26:13
The sluggard says, "There is a lion in the road! There is a lion in the streets!"

26:14
As a door turns on its hinges, so does a sluggard on his bed.

26:15
The sluggard buries his hand in the dish; it wears him out to bring it back to

26:12
Do you see a man who is wise in his own eyes? There is more hope for a fool than for him.
26:13
The sluggard says, "There is a lion in the road! There is a lion in the streets!"
26:14
As a door turns on its hinges, so does a sluggard on his bed.
26:15
The sluggard buries his hand in the dish; it wears him out to bring it back to

his mouth.

26:16

The sluggard is wiser in his own eyes than seven men who can answer discreetly.

26:17

He who meddles in a quarrel not his own is like one who takes a passing dog by the ears.

26:18

Like a madman who throws firebrands, arrows, and death,

26:19

is the man who deceives his neighbor and says,

his mouth.

26:16

The sluggard is wiser in his own eyes than seven men who can answer discreetly.

26:17

He who meddles in a quarrel not his own is like one who takes a passing dog by the ears.

26:18

Like a madman who throws firebrands, arrows, and death,

26:19

is the man who deceives his neighbor and says,

"I am only joking!"

26:20

For lack of wood the fire goes out; and where there is no whisperer, quarreling ceases.

26:21

As charcoal to hot embers and wood to fire, so is a quarrelsome man for kindling strife.

26:22

The words of a whisperer are like delicious morsels; they go down into the inner parts of the body.

26:23

Like the glaze covering an

"I am only joking!"

26:20

For lack of wood the fire goes out; and where there is no whisperer, quarreling ceases.

26:21

As charcoal to hot embers and wood to fire, so is a quarrelsome man for kindling strife.

26:22

The words of a whisperer are like delicious morsels; they go down into the inner parts of the body.

26:23

Like the glaze covering an

earthen vessel are smooth
lips with an evil heart.
26:24
He who hates, dissembles
with his lips and harbors
deceit in his heart;
26:25
when he speaks graciously,
believe him not, for there
are seven abominations in
his heart;
26:26
though his hatred be
covered with guile, his
wickedness will be exposed
in the assembly.
26:27
He who digs a pit will fall

earthen vessel
are smooth
lips with an
evil heart.
26:24
He who hates,
dissembles
with his lips
and harbors
deceit in his
heart;
26:25
when he
speaks
graciously,
believe him
not, for there
are seven
abominations
in his heart;
26:26
though his
hatred be
covered with
guile, his
wickedness
will be
exposed in
the assembly.
26:27
He who digs a
pit will fall

into it, and a stone will
come back upon
him who starts it rolling.

26:28

A lying tongue hates its
victims, and a flattering
mouth works ruin.

Proberbs **27**

27:1

Do not boast about
tomorrow, for you do not
know what a day may
bring forth.

27:2

Let another praise you, and

into it, and a stone will come back upon him who starts it rolling.

26:28

A lying tongue hates its victims, and a flattering mouth works ruin.

Proberbs **27**

27:1

Do not boast about tomorrow, for you do not know what a day may bring forth.

27:2

Let another praise you, and

not your own mouth; a stranger, and not your own lips.

27:3

A stone is heavy, and sand is weighty, but a fool's provocation is heavier than both.

27:4

Wrath is cruel, anger is overwhelming; but who can stand before jealousy?

27:5

Better is open rebuke than hidden love.

27:6

Faithful are the wounds of a friend; profuse are the

not your own mouth; a stranger, and not your own lips.

27:3

A stone is heavy, and sand is weighty, but a fool's provocation is heavier than both.

27:4

Wrath is cruel, anger is overwhelming; but who can stand before jealousy?

27:5

Better is open rebuke than hidden love.

27:6

Faithful are the wounds of a friend; profuse are the

kisses of an enemy.

27:7

He who is sated loathes honey, but to one who is hungry everything bitter is sweet.

27:8

Like a bird that strays from its nest, is a man who strays from his home.

27:9

Oil and perfume make the heart glad, but the soul is torn by trouble.

27:10

Your friend, and your father's friend, do not forsake; and do not go to

kisses of an enemy.

27:7

He who is sated loathes honey, but to one who is hungry everything bitter is sweet.

27:8

Like a bird that strays from its nest, is a man who strays from his home.

27:9

Oil and perfume make the heart glad, but the soul is torn by trouble.

27:10

Your friend, and your father's friend, do not forsake; and do not go to

your brother's house in the day of your calamity.
Better is a neighbor who is near than a brother who is far away.

27:11
Be wise, my son, and make my heart glad, that I may answer him who reproaches me.

27:12
A prudent man sees danger and hides himself; but the simple go on, and suffer for it.

27:13
Take a man's

your brother's house in the day of your calamity.
Better is a neighbor who is near than a brother who is far away.

27:11
Be wise, my son, and make my heart glad, that I may answer him who reproaches me.

27:12
A prudent man sees danger and hides himself; but the simple go on, and suffer for it.

27:13
Take a man's
garment when

garment when he has given surety for a stranger, and hold him in pledge when he gives surety for foreigners.

27:14
He who blesses his neighbor with a loud voice, rising early in the morning, will be counted as cursing.

27:15
A continual dripping on a rainy day and a contentious woman are alike;

27:16
to restrain her is to restrain the wind or to

he has given surety for a stranger, and hold him in pledge when he gives surety for foreigners.

27:14
He who blesses his neighbor with a loud voice, rising early in the morning, will be counted as cursing.

27:15
A continual dripping on a rainy day and a contentious woman are alike;
27:16
to restrain her is to restrain the wind or to

grasp oil in one's right hand.

27:17
Iron sharpens iron, and one man sharpens another.

27:18
He who tends a fig tree will eat its fruit, and he who guards his master will be honored.

27:19
As in water face answers to face, so the mind of man reflects the man.

27:20
Sheol and Abaddon are never satisfied, and never satisfied are the eyes of man.

grasp oil in one's right hand.

27:17
Iron sharpens iron, and one man sharpens another.

27:18
He who tends a fig tree will eat its fruit, and he who guards his master will be honored.

27:19
As in water face answers to face, so the mind of man reflects the man.

27:20
Sheol and Abaddon are never satisfied, and never satisfied are the eyes of man.

27:21
The crucible is for silver,
and the furnace is for gold,
and a man is judged by
his praise.

27:22
Crush a fool in a mortar
with a pestle along with
crushed grain, yet his folly
will not depart from him.

27:23
Know well the condition of
your flocks, and give
attention to your herds;

27:24
for riches do not last for
ever; and does a crown
endure to all generations?

27:21
The crucible is for silver, and the furnace is for gold, and a man is judged by his praise.

27:22
Crush a fool in a mortar with a pestle along with crushed grain, yet his folly will not depart from him.

27:23
Know well the condition of your flocks, and give attention to your herds;

27:24
for riches do not last for ever; and does a crown endure to all generations?

27:25
When the grass is gone, and the new growth appears, and the herbage of the mountains is gathered,
27:26
the lambs will provide your clothing, and the goats the price of a field;
27:27
there will be enough goats' milk for your food, for the food of your household and maintenance for your maidens.

27:25
When the grass is gone, and the new growth appears, and the herbage of the mountains is gathered,
27:26
the lambs will provide your clothing, and the goats the price of a field;
27:27
there will be enough goats' milk for your food, for the food of your household and maintenance for your maidens.

Proberbs 28

28:1
The wicked flee when no one pursues, but the righteous are bold as a lion.

28:2
When a land transgresses it has many rulers; but with men of understanding and knowledge its stability will long continue.

28:3
A poor man who oppresses the poor is a beating rain that leaves no food.

28:4
Those who forsake the law

Proberbs 28

28:1
The wicked flee when no one pursues, but the righteous are bold as a lion.

28:2
When a land transgresses it has many rulers; but with men of understanding and knowledge its stability will long continue.

28:3
A poor man who oppresses the poor is a beating rain that leaves no food.

28:4
Those who forsake the law

praise the wicked, but those who keep the law strive against them.

28:5

Evil men do not understand justice, but those who seek the LORD understand it completely.

28:6

Better is a poor man who walks in his integrity than a rich man who is perverse in his ways.

28:7

He who keeps the law is a wise son, but a companion of gluttons shames his

praise the wicked, but those who keep the law strive against them.

28:5

Evil men do not understand justice, but those who seek the LORD understand it completely.

28:6

Better is a poor man who walks in his integrity than a rich man who is perverse in his ways.

28:7

He who keeps the law is a wise son, but a companion of gluttons shames his father.

28:8

He who augments his
wealth by interest and
increase gathers it for him
who is kind to th poor.

28:9

If one turns away his ear
from hearing the law, even
his prayer is an
abomination.

28:10

He who misleads the
upright into an evil way
will fall into his own pit;
but the blameless will have

father.

28:8
He who
augments his
wealth by
interest and
increase
gathers it for
him who is
kind to the
poor.
28:9
If one turns
away his ear
from hearing
the law, even
his prayer is
an
abomination.
28:10
He who
misleads the
upright into
an evil way
will fall into
his own pit;
but the
blameless will
have

a goodly inheritance.
28:11
A rich man is wise in his own eyes, but a poor man who has understanding will find him out.
28:12
When the righteous triumph, there is great glory; but when the wicked rise, men hide themselves.
28:13
He who conceals his transgressions will not prosper, but he who confesses and forsakes them will obtain mercy.

a goodly inheritance.
28:11
A rich man is wise in his own eyes, but a poor man who has understanding will find him out.
28:12
When the righteous triumph, there is great glory; but when the wicked rise, men hide themselves.
28:13
He who conceals his transgressions will not prosper, but he who confesses and forsakes them will obtain mercy.

28:14
Blessed is the man who fears the LORD always; but he who hardens his heart will fall into calamity.

28:15
Like a roaring lion or a charging bear is a wicked ruler over a poor people.

28:16
A ruler who lacks understanding is a cruel oppressor; but he who hates unjust gain will prolong his days.

28:17
If a man is burdened with the blood of another, let

28:14
Blessed is the man who fears the LORD always; but he who hardens his heart will fall into calamity.

28:15
Like a roaring lion or a charging bear is a wicked ruler over a poor people.

28:16
A ruler who lacks understanding is a cruel oppressor; but he who hates unjust gain will prolong his days.

28:17
If a man is burdened with the blood of another, let

him be a fugitive until death; let no one help him.

28:18

He who walks in integrity will be delivered, but he who is perverse in his ways will fall into a pit.

28:19

He who tills his land will have plenty of bread, but he who follows worthless pursuits will have plenty of poverty.

28:20

A faithful man will abound with blessings, but he who hastens to be rich will not

him be a fugitive until death; let no one help him.

28:18

He who walks in integrity will be delivered, but he who is perverse in his ways will fall into a pit.

28:19

He who tills his land will have plenty of bread, but he who follows worthless pursuits will have plenty of poverty.

28:20

A faithful man will abound with blessings, but he who hastens to be rich will not go unpunished.

28:21

To show partiality is not good; but for a piece of bread a man will do wrong.

28:22

A miserly man hastens after wealth, and does not know that want will come upon him.

28:23

He who rebukes a man will afterward find more favor than he who flatters with his tongue.

28:24

He who robs his father or

go
unpunished.
28:21
To show partiality is not good; but for a piece of bread a man will do wrong.
28:22
A miserly man hastens after wealth, and does not know that want will come upon him.
28:23
He who rebukes a man will afterward find more favor than he who flatters with his tongue.
28:24
He who robs his father or his mother

his mother and says, "That is no transgression," is the companion of a man who destroys.

28:25

A greedy man stirs up strife, but he who trusts in the LORD will be enriched.

28:26

He who trusts in his own mind is a fool; but he who walks in wisdom will be delivered.

28:27

He who gives to the poor will not want, but he who hides his eyes will get

and says, "That is no transgression," is the companion of a man who destroys.

28:25

A greedy man stirs up strife, but he who trusts in the LORD will be enriched.

28:26

He who trusts in his own mind is a fool; but he who walks in wisdom will be delivered.

28:27

He who gives to the poor will not want, but he who hides his eyes will get

many a curse.
28:28
When the wicked rise, men hide themselves, but when they perish, the righteous increase.

Proberbs 29
29:1
He who is often reproved, yet stiffens his neck, will suddenly be broken beyond healing.
29:2
When the righteous are in authority, the people rejoice; but

many a curse.
28:28
When the wicked rise, men hide themselves, but when they perish, the righteous increase.

Proberbs 29
29:1
He who is often reproved, yet stiffens his neck, will suddenly be broken beyond healing.
29:2
When the righteous are in authority, the people rejoice; but

when the wicked rule, the people groan.

when the wicked rule, the people groan.

29:3

He who loves wisdom makes his father glad, but one who keeps company with harlots squanders his substance.

29:3

He who loves wisdom makes his father glad, but one who keeps company with harlots squanders his substance.

29:4

By justice a king gives stability to the land, but one who exacts gifts ruins it.

29:4

By justice a king gives stability to the land, but one who exacts gifts ruins it.

29:5

A man who flatters his neighbor spreads a net for his feet.

29:5

A man who flatters his neighbor spreads a net for his feet.

29:6

An evil man is ensnared in his transgression, but a righteous man sings and rejoices.

29:7

A righteous man knows the rights of the poor; a wicked man does not understand such knowledge.

29:8

Scoffers set a city aflame, but wise men turn away wrath.

29:9

If a wise man has an argument with a fool, the fool only rages and laughs,

29:6

An evil man is ensnared in his transgression, but a righteous man sings and rejoices.

29:7

A righteous man knows the rights of the poor; a wicked man does not understand such knowledge.

29:8

Scoffers set a city aflame, but wise men turn away wrath.

29:9

If a wise man has an argument with a fool, the fool only rages andlaughs, and

and there is no quiet.

29:10
Bloodthirsty men hate one who is blameless, and the wicked seek his life.

29:11
A fool gives full vent to his anger, but a wise man quietly holds it back.

29:12
If a ruler listens to falsehood, all his officials will be wicked.

29:13
The poor man and the oppressor meet together; the LORD gives light to

there is no quiet.

29:10
Bloodthirsty men hate one who is blameless, and the wicked seek his life.

29:11
A fool gives full vent to his anger, but a wise man quietly holds it back.

29:12
If a ruler listens to falsehood, all his officials will be wicked.

29:13
The poor man and the oppressor meet together; the LORD gives light to

the eyes of both.

29:14

If a king judges the poor with equity his throne will be established for ever.

29:15

The rod and reproof give wisdom, but a child left to himself brings shame to his mother.

29:16

When the wicked are in authority, transgression increases; but the righteous will look upon their downfall.

29:17

Discipline your son, and he

the eyes of both.

29:14

If a king judges the poor with equity his throne will be established for ever.

29:15

The rod and reproof give wisdom, but a child left to himself brings shame to his mother.

29:16

When the wicked are in authority, transgression increases; but the righteous will look upon their downfall.

29:17

Discipline your son, and he

will give you rest; he will give delight to your heart.

29:18

Where there is no prophecy the people cast off restraint, but blessed is he who keeps the law.

29:19

By mere words a servant is not disciplined, for though he understands, he will not give heed.

29:20

Do you see a man who is hasty in his words? There is more hope for a fool than for him.

will give you rest; he will give delight to your heart.

29:18

Where there is no prophecy the people cast off restraint, but blessed is he who keeps the law.

29:19

By mere words a servant is not disciplined, for though he understands, he will not give heed.

29:20

Do you see a man who is hasty in his words? There is more hope for a fool than for him.

29:21
He who pampers his servant from childhood, will in the end find him his heir.

29:22
A man of wrath stirs up strife, and a man given to anger causes much transgression.

29:23
A man's pride will bring him low, but he who is lowly in spirit will obtain honor.

29:24
The partner of a thief hates his own life; he hears

29:21
He who pampers his servant from childhood, will in the end find him his heir.

29:22
A man of wrath stirs up strife, and a man given to anger causes much transgression.

29:23
A man's pride will bring him low, but he who is lowly in spirit will obtain honor.

29:24
The partner of a thief hates his own life; he hears

the curse, but discloses nothing.

29:25

The fear of man lays a snare, but he who trusts in the LORD is safe.

29:26

Many seek the favor of a ruler, but from the LORD a man gets justice.

29:27

An unjust man is an abomination to the righteous, but he whose way is straight is an abomination to the wicked.

the curse, but discloses nothing.

29:25

The fear of man lays a snare, but he who trusts in the LORD is safe.

29:26

Many seek the favor of a ruler, but from the LORD a man gets justice.

29:27

An unjust man is an abomination to the righteous, but he whose way is straight is an abomination to the wicked.

Proberbs 30

30:1

The words of Agur son of Jakeh of Massa. The man says to Ith'i-el, to Ith'i-el and Ucal:

30:2

Surely I am too stupid to be a man. I have not the understanding of a man.

30:3

I have not learned wisdom, nor have I knowledge of the Holy One.

30:4

Who has ascended to heaven and come down? Who has gathered the wind

Proberbs 30
30:1
The words of Agur son of Jakeh of Massa. The man says to Ith'i-el, to Ith'i-el and Ucal:
30:2
Surely I am too stupid to be a man. I have not the understanding of a man.
30:3
I have not learned wisdom, nor have I knowledge of the Holy One.
30:4
Who has ascended to heaven and come down? Who has gathered the wind

in his fists? Who has wrapped up the waters in a garment? Who has established all the ends of the earth? What is his name, and what is his son's name? Surely you know!

30:5
Every word of God proves true; he is a shield to those who take refuge in him.

30:6
Do not add to his words, lest he rebuke you, and

in his fists? Who has wrapped up the waters in a garment? Who has established all the ends of the earth? What is his name, and what is his son's name? Surely you know!

30:5
Every word of God proves true; he is a shield to those who take refuge in him.

30:6
Do not add to his words, lest he rebuke you, and

you be found a liar.

30:7

Two things I ask of thee; deny them not to me before I die:

30:8

Remove far from me falsehood and lying; give me neither poverty nor riches; feed me with the food that is needful for me,

30:9

lest I be full, and deny thee, and say, "Who is the LORD?" or lest I be poor, and steal, and profane the name of my God.

you be found a liar.

30:7

Two things I ask of thee; deny them not to me before I die:

30:8

Remove far from me falsehood and lying; give me neither poverty nor riches; feed me with the food that is needful for me,

30:9

lest I be full, and deny thee, and say, "Who is the LORD?" or lest I be poor, and steal, and profane the name of my God.

30:10
Do not slander a servant to his master, lest he curse you, and you be held guilty.

30:11
There are those who curse their fathers and do not bless their mothers.

30:12
There are those who are pure in their own eyes but are not cleansed of their filth.

30:13
There are those - how lofty are their eyes, how high their eyelids lift!

30:10
Do not slander a servant to his master, lest he curse you, and you be held guilty.

30:11
There are those who curse their fathers and do not bless their mothers.

30:12
There are those who are pure in their own eyes but are not cleansed of their filth.

30:13
There are those - how lofty are their eyes, how high their eyelids lift!

30:14
There are those whose teeth are swords, whose teeth are knives, to devour the poor from off the earth, the needy from among men.
30:15
The leech has two daughters; "Give, give," they cry. Three things are never satisfied; four never say, "Enough":
30:16
Sheol, the barren womb, the earth ever thirsty for water, and the fire which never says, "Enough."

30:14
There are those whose teeth are swords, whose teeth are knives, to devour the poor from off the earth, the needy from among men.
30:15
The leech has two daughters; "Give, give," they cry. Three things are never satisfied; four never say, "Enough":
30:16
Sheol, the barren womb, the earth ever thirsty for water, and the fire which never says, "Enough."

30:17
The eye that mocks a father and scorns to obey a mother will be picked out by the ravens of the valley and eaten by the vultures.
30:18
Three things are too wonderful for me; four I do not understand:
30:19
the way of an eagle in the sky, the way of a serpent on a rock, the way of a ship on the high seas, and the way of a man with a maiden.

30:17
The eye that mocks a father and scorns to obey a mother will be picked out by the ravens of the valley and eaten by the vultures.
30:18
Three things are too wonderful for me; four I do not understand:
30:19
the way of an eagle in the sky, the way of a serpent on a rock, the way of a ship on the high seas, and the way of a man with a maiden.

30:20
This is the way of an adulteress: she eats, and wipes her mouth, and says, "I have done no wrong."
30:21
Under three things the earth trembles; under four it cannot bear up:
30:22
a slave when he becomes king, and a fool when he is filled with food;
30:23
an unloved woman when she gets a husband, and a maid when she succeeds

30:20
This is the way of an adulteress: she eats, and wipes her mouth, and says, "I have done no wrong."
30:21
Under three things the earth trembles; under four it cannot bear up:
30:22
a slave when he becomes king, and a fool when he is filled with food;
30:23
an unloved woman when she gets a husband, and a maid when she succeeds

her mistress.

30:24
Four things on earth are small, but they are exceedingly wise:

30:25
the ants are a people not strong, yet they provide their food in the summer;

30:26
the badgers are a people not mighty, yet they make their homes in the rocks;

30:27
the locusts have no king, yet all of them march in rank;

her mistress.

30:24
Four things on earth are small, but they are exceedingly wise:

30:25
the ants are a people not strong, yet they provide their food in the summer;

30:26
the badgers are a people not mighty, yet they make their homes in the rocks;

30:27
the locusts have no king, yet all of them march in rank;

30:28
the lizard you can take in your hands, yet it is in kings' palaces.

30:29
Three things are stately in their tread; four are stately in their stride:

30:30
the lion, which is mightiest among beasts and does not turn back before any;

30:31
the strutting cock, the he-goat, and a king striding before his people.

30:32
If you have been foolish,

30:28
the lizard you can take in your hands, yet it is in kings' palaces.

30:29
Three things are stately in their tread; four are stately in their stride:

30:30
the lion, which is mightiest among beasts and does not turn back before any;

30:31
the strutting cock, the he-goat, and a king striding before his people.

30:32
If you have been foolish,

exalting yourself, or if you
have been devising evil, put
your hand on your mouth.

30:33

For pressing milk produces
curds, pressing the nose
produces blood, and
pressing anger produces
strife.

Proberbs 31

31:1

The words of Lemuel, king
of Massa, which his mother
taught him:

31:2

What, my son? What,

exalting yourself, or if you have been devising evil, put your hand on your mouth.

30:33

For pressing milk produces curds, pressing the nose produces blood, and pressing anger produces strife.

Proberbs 31

31:1

The words of Lemuel, king of Massa, which his mother taught him:

31:2

What, my son? What,

son of my womb? What, son of my vows?

31:3

Give not your strength to women, your ways to those who destroy kings.

31:4

It is not for kings, O Lemuel, it is not for kings to drink wine, or for rulers to desire strong drink;

31:5

lest they drink and forget what has been decreed, and pervert the rights of all the afflicted.

31:6

Give strong drink to him

son of my womb? What. son of my vows?

31:3

Give not your strength to women, your ways to those who destroy kings.

31:4

It is not for kings, O Lemuel. it is not for kings to drink wine, or for rulers to desire strong drink;

31:5

lest they drink and forget what has been decreed, and pervert the rights of all the afflicted.

31:6

Give strong drink to him

who is perishing, and wine to those in bitter distress;

31:7
let them drink and forget their poverty, and remember their misery no more.

31:8
Open your mouth for the dumb, for the rights of all who are left desolate.

31:9
Open your mouth, judge righteously, maintain the rights of the poor and needy.

31:10
A good wife who can find? She is far more precious

who is perishing, and wine to those in bitter distress;

31:7
let them drink and forget their poverty, and remember their misery no more.

31:8
Open your mouth for the dumb, for the rights of all who are left desolate.

31:9
Open your mouth, judge righteously, maintain the rights of the poor and needy.

31:10
A good wife who can find? She is far more precious

than jewels.

31:11

The heart of her husband trusts in her, and he will have no lack of gain.

31:12

She does him good, and not harm, all the days of her life.

31:13

She seeks wool and flax, and works with willing hands.

31:14

She is like the ships of the merchant, she brings her food from afar.

than jewels.

31:11

The heart of her husband trusts in her, and he will have no lack of gain.

31:12

She does him good, and not harm, all the days of her life.

31:13

She seeks wool and flax, and works with willing hands.

31:14

She is like the ships of the merchant, she brings her food from afar.

31:15
She rises while it is yet night and provides food for her household and tasks for her maidens.

31:16
She considers a field and buys it; with the fruit of her hands she plants a vineyard.

31:17
She girds her loins with strength and makes her arms strong.

31:18
She perceives that her merchandise is profitable. Her lamp does not go out

31:15
She rises while it is yet night and provides food for her household and tasks for her maidens.

31:16
She considers a field and buys it; with the fruit of her hands she plants a vineyard.

31:17
She girds her loins with strength and makes her arms strong.

31:18
She perceives that her merchandise is profitable. Her lamp does not go out

at night.

31:19

She puts her hands to the distaff, and her hands hold the spindle.

31:20

She opens her hand to the poor, and reaches out her hands to the needy.

31:21

She is not afraid of snow for her household, for all her household are clothed in scarlet.

31:22

She makes herself coverings; her clothing is fine linen and purple.

at night.

31:19

She puts her hands to the distaff, and her hands hold the spindle.

31:20

She opens her hand to the poor, and reaches out her hands to the needy.

31:21

She is not afraid of snow for her household, for all her household are clothed in scarlet.

31:22

She makes herself coverings; her clothing is fine linen and purple.

31:23
Her husband is known in the gates, when he sits among the elders of the land.

31:24
She makes linen garments and sells them; she delivers girdles to the merchant.

31:25
Strength and dignity are her clothing, and she laughs at the time to come.

31:26
She opens her mouth with wisdom, and the teaching of kindness is on her tongue.

31:23
Her husband is known in the gates, when he sits among the elders of the land.

31:24
She makes linen garments and sells them; she delivers girdles to the merchant.

31:25
Strength and dignity are her clothing, and she laughs at the time to come.

31:26
She opens her mouth with wisdom, and the teaching of kindness is on her tongue.

31:27
She looks well to the ways of her household, and does not eat the bread of idleness.

31:28
Her children rise up and call her blessed; her husband also, and he praises her:

31:29
"Many women have done excellently, but you surpass them all."

31:30
Charm is deceitful, and beauty is vain, but a woman who fears the

31:27
She looks well to the ways of her household, and does not eat the bread of idleness.

31:28
Her children rise up and call her blessed; her husband also, and he praises her:

31:29 "Many women have done excellently, but you surpass them all."

31:30
Charm is deceitful, and beauty is vain, but a woman who fears the

LORD is to be praised.

31:31

Give her of the fruit of her hands, and let her works praise her in the gates.

LORD is to be praised.

31:31

Give her of the fruit of her hands, and let her works praise her in the gates.

판 권 지

필사 영어로 배우는

지혜의 책 잠언

저 : 서 미 미

초판 1 쇄 2021년 3 월 25일

편 낸 이 : 도서출판 保 惠

출판 등록 제2014-000001. 호 (2014.0103.)

주소 : 천안시 서북구 하리1길 39

전화 : 010-2239-0675

ISBN 979-11-87802-67-9

값17000원